PARENTING KIDS WITH ADD/ADHD: REAL TOOLS FOR REAL LIFE

By Dr. Al Winebarger, Ph.D.
Founder of the Grand Haven and Wyoming Attention Camps

FIRST EDITION

ARW Learning L.L.C.
Grand Haven, MI

ii

Library of Congress Catalog Card Number: 2004096004

ISBN: 0-9755545-0-6

ARW Learning L.L.C.
P.O. Box 18, Grand Haven, MI 49417
Phone (616) 842-4772 Fax (616) 842-5575
www.ARW.addr.com

COLLEGES, UNIVERSITIES, QUANTITY BUYERS:
Discounts on this book are available for bulk purchases.
Write or call for information on our discount programs.

TABLE OF CONTENTS

CHAPTER 1
ADD/ADHD Explained

ADD/ADHD Explained

Introduction

Welcome to the first chapter of our manual. This chapter will explain what ADD/ADHD is and how to tell if someone has ADD/ADHD. The chapter also gives a history of the disorder and will cover the three basic treatments for ADD/ADHD.

The *three basic treatment approaches* discussed in this chapter are:

> ➤ *Medication*

> ➤ *Behavior Management*

> ➤ *Medication Combined With Behavior Management*

This chapter will focus on giving you the tools you need to understand ADD/ADHD and the tools you will need to get your child assessed and treated.

Let's go to the next page and get started!

ROAD MAP TO CHAPTER 1

THINGS WE ARE GOING TO COVER IN THIS CHAPTER

We call this chapter *ADD/ADHD Explained* because we believe parents really need to understand what ADD/ADHD is before they try to help their kids. We want to explain ADD/ADHD in plain language, and to avoid "psycho-babble" at all costs!

The areas we will cover in this chapter are:

- *ADD/ADHD/HYPERACTIVITY*
  - *How long has ADD/ADHD been around?*
  - *What is ADD/ADHD anyway?*
- *HOW DO WE KNOW IF A KID HAS ADD/ADHD?*
  - *Assessment*
  - *Diagnosis*
- *THE BEST WAYS TO HELP KIDS WITH ADD/ADHD*
  - *Medications*
  - *Home and School Based Behavioral Strategies*

4

⑦ How Long Has ADD/ADHD Been Around? ⑦

The difficulties that come with ADD/ADHD probably have been around since the dawn of time – or at least since humans have been around! The disorder has been called many names, and has been defined in many different ways. Some definitions have been *pretty good* and some have been *dead wrong*.

The table below lists many of the names that have been used to describe this set of problems over the last 100-plus years.

A Brief History

1902 - "Deficits in moral control"

1930s-1960s - Minimal Brain Damage Syndrome

1930s - Hyperkinetic Impulse Disorder

1960s - Minimal Brain Dysfunction

1970s - Developmental Hyperactivity
    - Hyperkinetic Reaction to Childhood

1980 - Attention Deficit Disorder (ADD) with or without
    Hyperactivity (two separate types)

1987 - Attention Deficit Hyperactivity Disorder (ADHD)

1994 - Attention Deficit Hyperactivity Disorder
    (the definition currently in use – three types)
        ➤ Inattentive Type
        ➤ Impulsive Type
        ➤ Combined Type

So What Is ADHD Anyway?

General Description:

ADHD, Attention Deficit Hyperactivity Disorder, is a set of problems that may include *serious* trouble with *paying attention*, serious problems with *acting before thinking*, and/or serious problems caused by being *too active*. These difficulties start in early childhood; are usually long lasting; and are not due to some other problem such as brain damage, nervous system damage, mental retardation, a learning disability, or other emotional or behavior problems (like depression, anxiety, or oppositional behaviors). These difficulties almost always cause ***behavior challenges***, problems with learning and following rules, problems with maintaining efforts to achieve goals, problems with making and keeping friends, problems with school, and eventually to problems with job performance and maintaining relationships in adulthood.

6

Behavioral Challenges for Kids with ADD/ADHD

Kids with ADD/ADHD experience *Behavioral Challenges* that have their roots in the way their brains work. In general, these *Behavioral Challenges* fall into three groups:

SHOOTING FROM THE HIP,
PUTTING ON THE BRAKES, *and*
MISSING THE IMPORTANT THINGS

Part 1: SHOOTING FROM THE HIP

** **In many situations kids with ADD/ADHD have trouble with**

    ** **Acting *BEFORE* they think about the consequences**
          and
    ** **Acting *BEFORE* they decide if they want the consequences.**

EXAMPLE

> A parent tells a child with ADD/ADHD to take out the trash. The child says the first thing that pops into his/her head without *slowing down* to consider the consequences, blurting out "I don't want to!" without ever stopping to think about what might happen next. In other words, the kid SHOOTS FROM THE HIP and *gets in trouble!*

> SHOOTING FROM THE HIP robs children with ADHD of many opportunities to learn from behaviors, *without actually having to do them*. This happens when they don't **take the time** to make good decisions.

> "Time is the ultimate disability." (Barkley, 1998)

⬤ Behavioral Challenges for Kids with ADD/ADHD ⬤

Part 2: PUTTING ON THE BRAKES

Children with ADD/ADHD will often make the same mistake over and over again. Typically, this is the progression of how it happens:

1st **The kid does or says something.**

2nd **The kid begins to get into trouble with adults.**

3rd **The kid realizes that his/her behavior is not working.**

4th **The kid "gets it" that he or she is in trouble.**

5th **Despite being aware of being in trouble, the kid still has difficulty stopping.**

This represents a violation of what Dr. Al's granddad called the *First Rule of Holes*...

> ### *First Rule of Holes:*
> ## When you find yourself in one, STOP DIGGING!

Why do kids with ADD/ADHD do this? One of the main reasons is simply the difficulties caused by *SHOOTING FROM THE HIP*, as we discussed earlier. All of us struggle with *PUTTING ON THE BRAKES* when we are in trouble; it's even worse for kids who already have problems with not thinking things through and *SHOOTING FROM THE HIP*. These problems can cause things like impulsive lying, poor social behaviors, emotional difficulties, and increased problems with teachers and primary caregivers.

⚫ Behavioral Challenges for Kids with ADD/ADHD ⚫

Part 3: MISSING THE IMPORTANT THINGS

We are constantly *bombarded* by the things going on around us. People are talking, lights are humming, computers and appliances are running, birds are chirping. Many of the things going on around us are *unimportant* and we *tune them out*. This is really hard for kids with ADD/ADHD to do, so they often end up noticing all the things that *don't* matter, and *MISSING THE IMPORTANT THINGS that do* matter*!*

EXAMPLE:

Because of struggling with their ability to "tune in" to important things, kids with ADD/ADHD often will miss many of the subtle consequences of life, such as:

* A *teacher* changes her or his voice inflection and tone as a way of telling the child to get back to work.
* The *teacher* smiles as a reward.
* A *parent* gives a command from another room.
* A *friend* steps back to create some personal space when the youngster is "coming on too strong."

If kids with ADD/ADHD don't notice such things, they can't be expected to respond to them. However, *the world gets really mad* at kids with ADD/ADHD because the world doesn't realize that they are *MISSING THE IMPORTANT THINGS!*

☹ THE IMPACT OF ADD/ADHD ON ALL ☹ ASPECTS OF A KID'S LIFE: RIPPLES IN THE POND

Think About This:

Picture a rock being thrown into the middle of a still, flat pond. The ripples spread out in all directions and upset all sorts of things – even those things far away from where the rock landed. Many of these disturbances are easy to see: plants move, waves splash, boats tied at the pier bob up and down. However, *a whole bunch of other things are going on beneath the surface.* The fish are scared, water below the surface becomes muddied with silt and dirt, frogs and tadpoles scurry away.

Difficulties with *SHOOTING FROM THE HIP, PUTTING ON THE BRAKES, and/or MISSING THE IMPORTANT THINGS* often create a large number of "ripples" in the lives of children with ADD/ADHD. Just like when a rock is thrown into a pond, *some of the problems are obvious* – school work goes unfinished, rules are broken, parents and teachers get angry, friends push the child away. However, *much of the damage is not so obvious.* Kids with ADD/ADHD may feel bad about themselves and may not like themselves. They may feel they cannot make good things happen in their lives no matter how hard they try, and they may believe no one likes them. This is a very hard and very sad place to be. ☹☹

Who Gets ADD/ADHD?

Estimates of the number of young people who have ADD/ADHD vary widely – between 1% and 20% of all children. The *best* estimates in the scientific literature suggest that *between 3 to 5%* of all kids have ADD/ADHD. It appears that more boys (about 9%) than girls (3.3%) will have these difficulties.

Why is there such a wide range of estimates? **One of the main reasons has to do with how hard it is to measure ADD/ADHD. Measurement is difficult for a couple of reasons. First, as you will remember from earlier pages,** *our understanding of ADD/ADHD keeps growing and changing*, **and so do the definitions we use for these difficulties. Second, it's really hard to measure ADD/ADHD because it** *really is a matter of degree*, **not a cut-and-dried case of "Yes, you have it" or "No, you don't have it."**

So we want to think about the *degree* to which any given child has more trouble with *SHOOTING FROM THE HIP, PUTTING ON THE BRAKES, and/or MISSING THE IMPORTANT THINGS* than other kids his or her age. Finally, we have to make sure that the difficulties *are not due to some other cause* such as a learning disability or other emotional or behavior problems.

❓ HOW DO WE KNOW IF A KID ❓ HAS ADD/ADHD?

ADD/ADHD is one of the *most over-diagnosed* and *misdiagnosed* childhood conditions. Many kids who are given the ADD/ADHD label really don't have ADD/ADHD. Many of them have other very real difficulties like problems with aggression, being oppositional, anxiety or depression, and/or learning disabilities.

The best way to make sure your child is not misdiagnosed is to see that he or she receives a *Good Assessment*. This will ensure that the right interventions and treatments are applied to the right problems.

What Should A Good ADD/ADHD Assessment Look Like? The best way to make sure that ADD/ADHD is not *over-diagnosed* or *misdiagnosed* is to use a three-part assessment process – the *Clinical Interview*, the use of *Psycho-Educational Testing* and the use of *Questionnaires*. Within those segments, any good assessment should include the following elements:

PARTS OF A GOOD ASSESSMENT

1. **CLINICAL INTERVIEW**
   - Parents — Experts on Their Own Kids
   - Child
   - Teachers (if possible) — Developmental Experts
2. **TESTING**
   - IQ
   - Achievement
   - Sustained Attention Task
3. **OBJECTIVE MEASURES**
   - Parent Report Measures — Global Snapshot of Behaviors Across Domains
   - Teacher Report Measures
   - Child Report Measures

* Please Note: If possible, it is also nice to directly observe the child at home and at school – but insurance companies usually won't cover this.

WHAT DOES ALL THIS INFORMATION TELL ME ABOUT MY KID AND ADD/ADHD?

Putting your child through a *Good Assessment* allows your family doctor, psychologist and/or psychiatrist to make sure they have the *Best Estimate Diagnosis*. They can *rule out mimicking problems* and create a *snapshot* of your child's *relative strengths and weaknesses*. This helps the professionals working with your child to form a good and useful treatment plan – one that can actually help you to help your child be more successful and to feel better about life.

WHAT HAPPENS WHEN YOU "SHORT-CUT" THIS PROCESS?

When we fail to collect enough information, our picture of the child in question can be very blurry – like this:

When we have a blurry picture a number of things can happen:

- ➢ Over-Diagnosis
- ➢ Over-Medication
- ➢ Problems Will Continue...and May Become Worse!

So be a *smart consumer* and make sure your family doctor and mental health professional know how to collect all the information they need. The best way to find out is to ask them. GIVE THEM A QUIZ! Please refer to the Appendix in the back of the book for a list of suggested questions. If they can't pass your quiz – pass on them!

TREATMENT FOR ADHD – WHERE DO WE GO FROM HERE?

So the child has gone through a *Good Assessment* and it appears that ADD/ADHD is the right diagnosis – *WHAT DO WE DO NOW?*

That is a *very good question*. The *three most useful* ways to treat ADD/ADHD, as determined by researchers over the last 30 years, are:

> *Medication*

> *Behavior Management*

> *Medication Combined With Behavior Management*

Our manual focuses on these three approaches because a large body of science has found them to be useful. A wide range of other approaches exist – everything from diet to "behavioral optometry." However, the scientific support for most of them is sketchy at best, so they are not presented here.

Please go on to the next page!

Medications – They Definitely Help
BUT THERE ARE NO MAGIC BULLETS

Given that ADD/ADHD truly appears to be based in the way the brain is wired, it is not surprising that medications have been found to be helpful in its treatment. In general, it's estimated that two-thirds to three-fourths of all kids who have ADD/ADHD will show some improvement when they take medication. The most commonly used medications are the *stimulants*. In low doses, stimulants help us focus – that's one of the reasons so many people get their daily dose of caffeine from drinking coffee in the morning! Such medications are generally believed to help kids with ADD/ADHD by stimulating the creation of brain chemicals (also called neurotransmitters) that help us be more sensitive to the consequences of our behaviors. Some of the more common stimulants are listed in the table on the next page.

A newer *non-stimulant medication*, called *Strattera®*, helps the brain make better use of the chemicals it already produces, rather than causing the brain to create more (like stimulants do). Finally, some *antidepressant medications* also have been found to be helpful with kids who have ADD/ADHD. These medications are also listed in the table on the next page.

Please go on to the next page!

Medications Commonly Used With ADD/ADHD

Stimulant medications:

>   Ritalin
>   Concerta®
>   Adderall XR®
>   Cylert®
>   Dexedrine®

Non-stimulant medications: (Norepinepherine Reuptake Inhibitor)
>   Strattera®

Antidepressant medications:
>   Tricyclic antidepressants:
>>   Desipramine
>>   Imipramine

>   Selective dopamine agonist:
>>   Wellbutrin XL™

>   Selective serotoninergic reuptake inhibitor (SSRI):
>>   Prozac®

>   Miscellaneous agents:
>>   Beta-adrenergic blockers and Clonidine

Medications **and their use** *should always be discussed with your family practice doctor, pediatrician and/or psychiatrist.* **It is often helpful to have your psychologist consult with these prescribing professionals – especially the psychologist who helped you with the assessment process.**

Other biological treatments: *Biofeedback* **(EEG and EMG) appears to be a promising additional biology-based treatment – look for future studies!**

Characteristics of Good Home and School Based
Behavior Management Approaches

In national studies, *Behavior Management* has been found to work about as well as medications. These approaches certainly assist kids who have problems with *SHOOTING FROM THE HIP, PUTTING ON THE BRAKES and/or MISSING THE IMPORTANT THINGS* by slowing them down, providing structure to their world, and helping them to notice their environment and learn from their consequences. In general, a good *Behavior Management Plan* is guided by the ideas listed in the table starting on the next page.

Figuring out what to do is hard!

Please go on to the next page!

General ADD/ADHD
Related Behavior Management Ideas

Over the last 30 years, experts working with children and families struggling with ADD/ADHD have found 10 common ideas to be the most useful in changing behaviors. They include the following:

1. Behavioral Interventions should focus on the management of the disability. Remember that ADD/ADHD is related to brain wiring – it's not going to go away.

2. Behavioral Plans should be adjusted as the kid gets older. What works for a 6-year-old may not work for a 16-year-old!

3. Don't assume that medication interventions "cure" the problems.
    * Medications *don't* make up for lost learning opportunities. *
    * Medications *do* set the stage for maximizing learning. *

4. Make the information kids need to manage their behaviors very noticeable. Use things like:
    ➢ Cues/Prompts
    ➢ Reminders
    ➢ Physical props
    ➢ Self-talk
    ➢ Watch alarms

5. Eliminate time gaps
    ➢ Between behaviors and consequences;
    ➢ Between behaviors and feedback;
    ➢ Between steps in the process (assignment and due dates, for example)

6. Emphasize the sense of time passing by using
   - ➢ Ticking timers
   - ➢ Watch alarms
   - ➢ Other timing devices

7. Externalize Sources of Motivation or Drive.
   - ➢ Use reward systems at school and home.
   - ➢ Apply motivators (rewards) at the point of performance.
   - ➢ Remember the following points:
     - * Self-generated/internal forms of motivation are often weak or ineffective;
     - * External motivators must happen when the behaviors happen – at the same time and place;
     - * Interventions must be sustainable for long periods;
     - * Don't discontinue when successes begin;
     - * Customize motivators as the person matures.

8. Teach ways to solve problems in new or novel situations.
   - ➢ Have kids talk themselves through problems.
   - ➢ Help kids use skills they have learned in other settings.

9. Manage ADHD as a Chronic Disability.
   - ➢ Customize supports to account for increasing skills.
   - ➢ Avoid the complete removal of supports.
   - ➢ Educate and empower the person with ADHD.

10. Intervene across settings.
    - ➢ Coordinate efforts at school and home.
    - ➢ Make sure all adults are doing the same things to help.

THIS ALL SOUNDS VERY GOOD – BUT HOW DO WE ACCOMPLISH THESE THINGS?
THE ONLY WAY TO BE SUCCESSFUL
IS THROUGH THE TEAM APPROACH!

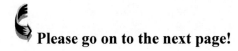 **Please go on to the next page!**

KEYS TO WORKING TOGETHER AS A TEAM

How do we work together as a team? It is often the case that by the time a psychologist or behavioral consultant gets involved, parents and caregivers are mad at teachers, teachers are frustrated with parents and caregivers, and everyone is frustrated with the kids. The following five steps will help you build a successful team to help your child.

1. MAINTAIN *OPEN COMMUNICATION*

    Everyone working with your child needs to be able to communicate with everyone else on a regular basis. This can take the form of talking in person, talking on the phone or using a daily school report card. (These are covered in the next chapter.) Most important, this communication needs to be *easy*, *frequent*, and *convenient*.

2. DON'T ALLOW *TURF ISSUES* TO GET IN THE WAY

    A *TURF ISSUE* occurs whenever anyone feels they are being told what to do by people who do not have the right to do so, or by people who do not understand what is happening. For example, a parent may resent suggestions about things to do at home from a classroom teacher, or a teacher may resent advice about how to cope with the child in the classroom from the family physician, the clinical psychologist or the parent/caregiver. *Don't let this happen!* Consider ideas from everyone and be understanding!

KEYS TO WORKING TOGETHER AS A TEAM
(Continued)

3. *UNDERSTAND* THE **FRUSTRATION OF OTHER PEOPLE**

We know that coping with the difficulties and behavior challenges created by ADD/ADHD can be difficult and frustrating at times. Try to be supportive of one another, and try to understand that the frustration of other adults is almost always based in the desire to do what's best for your child.

4. *TRUST YOUR EXPERTS*

Everyone needs to remember and value the skills and "know-how" present in the members of the team working with the child. Remember that:

- *PARENTS* ARE EXPERTS ON THEIR CHILD

- *TEACHERS* ARE DEVELOPMENTAL EXPERTS

- *PHYSICIANS* ARE EXPERTS ON THE USE OF MEDICINE

- *PSYCHOLOGISTS/THERAPISTS* ARE BEHAVIORAL EXPERTS

5. *AVOID "TAKING THINGS PERSONALLY"*

Everyone needs to remember the three causes of the behavioral challenges faced by kids with ADHD/ADD: *SHOOTING FROM THE HIP, PUTTING ON THE BRAKES and/or MISSING THE IMPORTANT THINGS.* If you remember these things, you won't personalize the problems and things will only be as hard as they have to be!

6. *COORDINATE YOUR EFFORTS*

If we fail at Nos. 1-5 above, the child pays! In other words, if we cannot work together, the only person who will suffer will be the child. Remember to keep in mind that every member of the team working with your child wants her or him to succeed and wants your child to be as happy and as healthy as they can possibly be!

Chapter Summary/Preview of Chapter 2

This chapter has covered a lot of ground and has thrown many new ideas at you. If anything presented in this chapter is unclear, please try to meet with your psychologist, physician or social worker to discuss the issues you don't understand. Also, feel free to drop us a line at DocAl@charter.net if you have any questions for Dr. Al.

Note from Dr. Al: Now that you have a good understanding of what ADD/ADHD is and the causes of the behavioral challenges faced by children with this condition, the next chapter will take you through *The Nuts and Bolts of Behavior Management*. We have made every attempt to make the chapter helpful and "user-friendly." After reading the next chapter, we encourage you to discuss the ideas it contains with your psychologist or other behavioral expert and consider the ways that you may be able to use those ideas with your own child.

Chapter 2 Will Focus On The Following Tools:

- Ways to prevent problems before they start
- Ways to change behaviors through using *Clear Requests*
- Targeting *Behavior Goals* by using Tracking Forms and Point Charts
- The nuts and bolts of building a Point Chart to use with your child
- Linking rewards and consequences to daily Point Chart Goals

CHAPTER 2
The Nuts and Bolts of Behavior Management: Teaching New Behaviors to Kids With ADD/ADHD

THE NUTS AND BOLTS OF BEHAVIOR CHANGE

Introduction

In the last chapter we learned about ADD/ADHD and the problems faced by kids and families who struggle with it every day. In Chapter 1 we covered the three basic treatments for ADD/ADHD.

The *three basic treatment approaches* outlined in Chapter 1 are:

> ➢ *Medication*

> ➢ *Behavior Management*

> ➢ *Medication Combined With Behavior Management*

This chapter will focus on *Behavior Management* and will teach you some basic ways to help kids with ADD/ADHD change their behaviors and be more successful at school, home, and with their friends.

This chapter *will not* discuss the use of medications. Please see Chapter 1 for a brief discussion of medications and/or discuss the use of medications with your pediatrician, family doctor, or a psychiatrist. Once you fully understand the use of *Behavioral Interventions and Treatments*, we suggest that you talk with a local psychologist or mental health professional and your family doctor or pediatrician if you are interested in designing a program that *combines Medication and Behavioral Approaches.*

ROAD MAP TO CHAPTER 2

THINGS WE ARE GOING TO COVER IN THIS CHAPTER

- Ways to prevent problems before they start

- Ways to change behaviors through using *Clear Requests*

- Targeting *Behavior Goals* by using Tracking Forms and Point Charts

- The nuts and bolts of building a Point Chart to use with your child

- *Linking* rewards and consequences to daily Point Chart goals

STEPS TO NEW WAYS OF TEACHING KIDS WHAT WE WANT THEM TO LEARN

The Importance of Preventing Problems Before They Start

 Think About This: **A famous poem tells a story about a village that sits on the edge of a cliff. Day after day people are injured by falling off the cliff into the valley below.**

A village meeting is held to discuss ways to solve the problem, and two possible solutions emerge:

> ➤ *Build a fence;*

> ➤ *Keep an ambulance in the valley!*

When dealing with kids with ADD/ADHD, we tend to *keep an ambulance in the valley*. In other words, we put a lot of effort into solving problems *after* they start. We must *avoid doing this* if we can!

So the first step to successful teaching is to Prevent Problems *before* they begin. One of the easiest ways to do this is to use *Clear Requests*.

Clear Requests – An Ounce of Prevention

The use of *Clear Requests* will help us avoid confusion due to misunderstanding and lessen the problems kids with ADHD have with *SHOOTING FROM THE HIP, PUTTING ON THE BRAKES* and *MISSING THE IMPORTANT THINGS* that so often cause them difficulties at home, at school and in life. Let's go on to the next page to learn how to make *Clear Requests*.

✴ STEPS TO MAKING CLEAR REQUESTS: ✴
A "HOW TO DO IT" GUIDE TO PREVENTION

This section is the "how to" guide for what is probably the single most important teaching tool you can use as a parent. This is true for the parents of kids in general, and especially true for the parents of kids with ADD/ADHD.

The table below lists the steps in making *Clear Requests*. Each step in the process is briefly explained on the next several pages. Once you have read these pages, *please practice* the steps repeatedly with another adult before you try using them with your kids. Being really good at making *Clear Requests* is essential – as the old saying goes, if you can't do this, everything else in this chapter will be like "re-arranging deck chairs on the Titanic." The other steps won't matter and they probably won't work. So PLEASE PRACTICE!

Making Clear Requests: 8 Steps to Success

1. Make Eye Contact.

2. Keep Your Voice Calm.

3. Be Specific and Avoid Questions. (Eliminate Wiggle Room!)

4. Use "Do It" Instead of "Stop It" Requests.

5. Give Only One Direction at a Time.

6. Encourage a Job Well Done – REWARD!

7. Avoid Negative Trailers!

8. Wait 10 Seconds.

♥ Making Clear Requests: 8 Steps to Success Explained ♥

The following pages explain each step involved in making *Clear Requests*. Please read each step, then think about ways to use each step with your child. Remember, *practicing is really important!*

1. <u>*Make Eye Contact*</u>: We spend a lot of time talking to the tops, sides and backs of kids' heads. If *we don't have their eyes*, we probably *don't have their attention*. If we don't have their attention, then they may be *MISSING IMPORTANT THINGS!* Consider having the following family rule: Any time you talk to someone, make sure you are both in the same room!

♥ ♥ ♥ ♥ ♥

2. <u>*Keep Your Voice Calm*</u>: Kids will match our tone! If we use an angry tone, they will most likely become angry too – and this is really true for kids who have trouble with *SHOOTING FROM THE HIP and PUTTING ON THE BRAKES*. Angry and frustrated tones simply make things harder than they have to be.

♥ ♥ ♥ ♥ ♥

3. <u>*Be Specific and Avoid Questions:*</u> (Eliminate Wiggle Room!) This is one of the hardest steps for parents. Remember, if you are not clear and specific, your child may choose to misunderstand or *may truly not*

understand what you want. Be polite, not passive. Only ask questions if you need information or if you are willing to live with all possible answers.

💡💡💡💡💡

4. <u>*Use "Do It" Instead of "Stop It" Requests*</u>: This means you should tell the child what to do. Many of the commands we give kids are "Stop it" or "Knock it off" commands, such as "Stop yelling at me!" That only tells kids WHAT NOT TO DO. "Do it" commands such as "Talk to me in a polite voice" tells kids WHAT TO DO.

💡💡💡💡💡

5. <u>*Give Only One Direction at a Time*</u>: Only give two-part commands if you're sure your kid can handle them. Remember, kids with ADHD often get distracted and will drift off in the middle of jobs that have several unrelated parts.

💡💡💡💡💡

6. <u>*Encourage a Job Well Done – REWARD!*</u> Often the best reward is simple praise. Remember to make eye contact when you praise – we need to get our kids' attention when we are praising them, just like we need to get their attention when we tell them to do things. So don't forget to maintain eye contact!

☺ Remember – we need to praise more often than discipline! ☺

30

7. *Avoid Negative Trailers!* **This is an example of a negative trailer: "Good job making your bed! Now why can't you do that all the time? We wouldn't have these problems if you would just do this all the time, #@&*\$!" Would you feel praised or punished if this was said to you? If you are adding negative trailers, your stress level is probably too high. Please see Chapter 5, "What to Do When the Kids Are Driving You Nuts," for some helpful hints on managing stress.**

8. *Wait 10 Seconds:* **Let's give our kids a chance to obey! Average kids need at least 5 seconds to stop what they are doing and begin doing what we tell them to do. If we go too fast, our kids with ADHD are most certainly going to** *SHOOT FROM THE HIP* **and have trouble with** *PUTTING ON THE BRAKES!*

 Using the eight steps to making *Clear Requests* **should decrease the overall stress level in your family, increase the number of times things go well in your family, and really help elevate your kid's self-esteem. Dr. Al works on this set of skills every day in his personal** *and* **professional life. It's truly worth the effort!**

Please turn the page!

KEEPING TRACK OF WHAT OUR KIDS DO – THE KEY TO TEACHING

Before deciding what we want to teach our kids to do, we need to know what they are already capable of doing and what they don't know how to do! We also need a way to *keep track* **of when they are trying to change their behaviors, when their behaviors actually do change, and times when they are not trying to make positive changes.** *TRACKING FORMS (things like Star Charts and Point Charts)* **help us to accomplish this. What do** *TRACKING FORMS* **do for us?**

1. *TRACKING FORMS* help us **NOTICE** what our kids are really doing.

   ☆ They help us **notice** the things going on around your family.

   ☆ They make sure we don't **miss many of the things** our kids do.

      ☆ **For example:** Adolescent felons "mind" 40-50% of the time, but it usually goes unnoticed because they are so extreme the rest of the time and there is no system to keep track of the times they are good!

2. *TRACKING FORMS* (Star Charts, Point Charts, etc.) **PROVIDE STRUCTURE.**

   ☆ As we said above, they **help us notice** the things our kids do.

   ☆ They **help us teach** our kids by giving us a tool to provide feedback like:

      ☆ *Rewards*
      ☆ *Discipline/Negative Consequences*

   ☆ They help us **slow the world down** so learning can happen. This should help with the problems kids with ADD/ADHD have with *SHOOTING FROM THE HIP, PUTTING ON THE BRAKES and/or MISSING THE IMPORTANT THINGS!*

   ☆ They keep us from getting into the habit of **"letting sleeping dogs lie"** – that is, only talking to our kids when they are in trouble!

32

 TRACKING FORMS AS CONTRACTS
and
CONTRACTS AS TEACHING TOOLS

1. Parents use contracts and tracking forms all the time. A contract is simply an agreement between you and your child. It lets everyone know what is expected of them, what the benefits will be for honoring the contract (rewards for following the rules), and what the consequences will be for failing to honor the contract (discipline for not doing your chores). What a great way to learn a good work ethic!

2. Parents usually use two types of contracts – informal and formal . We will describe both types below:

Informal Contracts: These are contracts that are simply spoken and not written down.

    Example #1: "You may watch TV after you feed the dog."
    Example #2: "You may play if the table is set."

As you can see, a clear "If → Then" situation has been created. However, it is simply spoken and *must be remembered by both* the kid and the parent.

Formal Contracts: These are contracts that are *written down*. They help us avoid misunderstandings due to forgetting, disagreeing or other causes.

    Example #1: *Star Charts* for younger kids
    Example #2: *Point Charts* for older kids

The Point Chart on the next page shows a typical formal contract, where all the kid's expectations are written down, and broken down into "do-able" steps. This will help our kids to build the important connections between the things they do and the consequences they get!

☺☺☺☺☺☺☺☺☺☺☺☺

A SAMPLE POINT CHART

Date:

	Sun	Mon	Tues	Wed	Thurs	Fri	Sat
Getting Ready for School (10 total) -Teeth (2) -Dressed (2) -Covers pulled up on bed (2) -Meds (4)							
Homework/Reading (20 total) (Right after dinner – before playing)							
School Agenda Book/ School Card (20 total) (Bringing it home)							
Picking Up Room (20 total) -Clothes in basket (4) -Dishes/food cleaned up (4) -Dresser drawers closed/top tidy (4) -Clothes folded (4) -Clear floor (4) (Before bed)							
Getting Ready for Bed (20 total) -Brushing teeth (5) -In bed by 9 (5) -Lights out by 10 (5) -Family room tidy (Put away toys and/or books) (5)							
Pleasant and Polite Attitude (10 total)							
Total	/100	/100	/100	/100	/100	/100	/100

Please go on to the next page for step-by-step instructions for building your own Point Chart.

33

34

STEPS TO USING POINT CHARTS TO HELP KIDS LEARN BY LINKING BEHAVIORS AND CONSEQUENCES

At this point, you may be thinking something like:

⑦ How exactly does a Point Chart teach anyway?

This section explains how Point Charts teach and gives you the step-by-step instructions you will need to create your own Point Chart. Just follow the steps marked by a 💡 to understand *how* **Point Charts work.**

💡 *First,* a Point Chart (like the one on the previous page) is created to use with your child.

💡 *Then* a daily goal is set.

💡 *If* the daily goal is met, *then* the child gets daily privileges.

💡 *If* the daily goal is not met, *then* the child does not get daily privileges.

💡 A *very noticeable connection* is formed, and learning takes place!

☆ **Remember that kids who struggle with ADD/ADHD miss many chances to learn because of their struggles with** *SHOOTING FROM THE HIP, PUTTING ON THE BRAKES and/or MISSING THE IMPORTANT THINGS.*

The structure and consequences of the Point Chart slows their world down enough to let learning happen. It causes the links between behaviors and consequences to be noticed. When these links are noticed, *three basic things happen*:

1. *Self-Esteem improves* as kids realize that they can change their consequences by changing their behaviors. This is very powerful and can help your kids to *keep trying even when the going gets tough.*

2. *Areas needing work* can be broken down into steps and the child can *feel good about the effort* being made, even when the outcome is not yet perfect. Kids really need to hear about the good things they do at least *5 times more often* than they hear about their mistakes! *5 TIMES MORE OFTEN!*

3. *Natural consequences occur.* Losing things like daily TV and video game privileges when the daily point goal is not met can be very effective. These things are much more powerful than words and much more effective than scolding or yelling or getting mad!

Please go on to the next page!

How to Build a Point Chart/Star Chart to Use With Your Child – It's Not As Hard As It Looks!

Now that we know what *Point/Star Charts* are and how they can be used to teach, how do we go about constructing one for your child?

The best way is to follow the steps listed on the next few pages. They contain the *nuts and bolts* steps you will need to start building a Point Chart or Star Chart to use with your child.

Please remember that this chapter is designed just to get you started; the issues with your child may require additional assistance from a qualified professional. If after reviewing this section you find yourself having trouble getting started, contact your local psychologist or behavioral expert – they should be able to get you going in no time!

So let's get on with learning how to build the Point Chart to use with your child!

Please go on to the next page!

Building a Point Chart/Star Chart
☺ **Let's Get Started!** ☺

☆ <u>**The First Step Is Picking the Place to Start**</u> ☆

Think about what your child does well. This is our foundation – *our place to start!* **Your child does many things well. However, it may be difficult to remember this at times. This may be most true when you are tired or frustrated. So begin by reminding yourself of the things your kids do that you like and that please you. Take a minute and write down a few of them:**

1. _____

2. _____

3. _____

4. _____

☆ <u>**The Second Step Is Deciding What You Would Like Your Child to Do Better**</u> ☆

Please list a couple of behaviors you don't like or areas in which you would like your child to improve. Please be as specific and as realistic as possible. (IMPORTANT: Avoid generalities like "Be Good." Goals like "Completing Homework" or "Cleaning His Room" might be good examples.)

1. _____

2. _____

3. _____

4. _____

Now let's go on to the next page to break it down even more!

★ *POINT CHART WORKSHEET* ★

Pick something from the last page that you would like to see improved and write it the space below. We'll call this our *Behavior Goal.* Then break down the Behavior Goal into very clear parts – make the parts so clear that strangers would understand them if they came to live in your home! Now transfer the Behavior Goal and its parts to your Point Chart. (Look in the Appendix to find a blank Point Chart you can use for this purpose!) Finally, think about the ways you plan to reward your child when he or she reaches the Behavior Goal. Repeat this process for each new Behavior Goal until you have completed your Point Chart. (Look at the Point Chart back on Page 33 for ideas if you are stuck.)

A. What I'd Like to Improve – the *Behavior Goal*:

B: List the parts of our *Behavior Goal.* (BE SPECIFIC!)

      1. _____

      2. _____

      3. _____

      4. _____

      5. _____

C. Transfer the *Behavior Goal and the steps* to the Point Chart.

This form should help you get the new behaviors broken down into steps to put on your Point Chart. Remember, there are more of these forms and a blank Point Chart in the Appendix – copy them and use them! ☺☺

TRANSFERING BEHAVIOR GOALS TO THE POINT CHART

Now that you have identified the *Behavior Goals* for your child and have broken them down into their parts, you can transfer them to the blank Point Chart contained in the Appendix or even create one on your own computer. You may also contact us at our Web site (www.wbc.addr.com) and we will send you electronic versions of examples and/or copies of blank Point Charts to use. To successfully transfer the *Behavior Goals*, simply follow the steps described below:

Step #1: Decide how many total points your child can earn each day. In general, you want to have *100 possible points per day* for your child to earn – this will remind them of the way that tests are graded in school. If you are building a Star Chart for younger children (under the age of 6), then you will want the total number of stars to add up to 10. This will make it easier for younger kids to understand.

Step #2: Assign point values to the *Behavior Goals*, and then assign values to each of the steps involved in them. For example, if "*Cleaning Your Room*" is a *Behavior Goal*, you might make it worth a total of 15 points. You then assign a point value to each step in "*Cleaning Your Room.*" (The steps already should be broken down on the worksheet from the previous

40

page.) When you transfer the *Behavior Goal* to a row on a Point Chart, it should look something like this:

 A Single Row From a Sample Point Chart

	Sun	Mon	Tues	Wed	Thurs	Fri	Sat

Cleaning Room (15 points)
  -Make bed (5 points)
  -Dirty clothes in hamper (5 points)
  -Toys off the floor (5 points)							

Listing each part of the *Behavior Goal* on the Point Chart is very important. Specifically, you want to make sure that your child gets credit *for attempting any part* of the *Behavior Goal*. As you can see from the example above, the steps the child has to complete and the value of each step are clearly listed on the chart. In this example, if only the first step (making the bed) is completed, then the child will receive 5 of the 15 possible points. If two steps are completed, the child would receive 10 points, and so on.

Breaking the *Behavior Goals* down into parts allows us to reward kids for the efforts they make, and to avoid "all or nothing" situations that may reduce their motivation to participate. What's more, when a child's daily privileges are linked to achieving a daily point goal, a very strong link will be made between the things they choose to do and the consequences they receive. In other words, this allows teaching to occur! Let's look at a step-by-step guide to accomplishing this.

 Please go on to the next page!

Linking the Point Chart to Privileges:
Giving Kids a Reason to Care

Remember the steps to using our Point Chart to teach:

- **A daily goal is set**: This should be about 60-80% of the points and/or stars possible (for example, if 100 points are possible each day, a good starting goal might be 70 points).

- **If the daily goal *is* met, *then* the child gets daily privileges**: Remember that watching TV, playing on the computer, playing with video games and going over to friends' houses are privileges – **NOT GOD GIVEN RIGHTS!** What we mean is, make sure your child *earns* the right to do these things; it's a life lesson that will serve him or her well. **Weekly rewards** (like a trip to the movies or a small toy) can be added when kids are hitting their daily goals regularly.

- **If the daily goal *is not* met, *then* the child does not get daily privileges**: Losing privileges often reminds kids to be motivated to meet their goals – or to earn their privileges!

- **A *very noticeable connection* is formed and learning takes place**! When this happens, children are happier, healthier and more successful!

School Cards – One Last Helpful Tool

School can often be a tough place for kids with ADD/ADHD. Kids who struggle with *SHOOTING FROM THE HIP, PUTTING ON THE BRAKES* and *MISSING THE IMPORTANT THINGS* frequently struggle with paying attention in class, work completion, turning in homework, dealing with teachers and staff, and making friends.

Unfortunately, parents and caregivers often don't find out about problems at school until they receive a call from a teacher or principal, the child is suspended, or a report card comes home. We believe that parents/caregivers need *daily* feedback about how their child with ADD/ADHD is doing at school. Waiting for a call from a teacher or for a report card is *WAITING TOO LONG*. Once a semester, quarter, marking period or even a week goes by, valuable time for teaching and changing behaviors has been lost.

School cards should be easy to use and should list areas of concern for your child with ADD/ADHD. Useful School Cards usually list things like:

> ➢ Being "On Task"
> ➢ Staying in your seat
> ➢ Following directions
> ➢ Being a "Good Friend"
> ➢ Work completion
> ➢ Overdue homework

School Cards are the perfect way to find out how your child is doing in school every day and can be added to the Point Chart you use with your child. (Please see the Point Chart on page 33.) Examples of School Cards are on the next page and in the Appendix at the end of this manual.

☆ SAMPLE SCHOOL CARDS ☆

 ## SCHOOL CARD FOR ELEMENTARY AGE STUDENTS

Date: _____

Goals	Before 10 a.m.	After 10 a.m.
On Task	☺ ☺	☺ ☺
Staying in seat when I'm supposed to	☺ ☺	☺ ☺
Getting along with others	☺ ☺	☺ ☺
Following directions	☺ ☺	☺ ☺

Note to teacher: Two ☺s = "Great job"; One ☺ = "Good, but could improve"; Zero ☺ = "Needs work"

SAMPLE SCHOOL CARD #2 – FOR USE WITH OLDER KIDS

NAME: DATE:

Class/Hour	On Time	Homework: Overdue?	Homework Assigned	On Task?	Teacher Initials and Comments
Geometry	YES / NO	YES / NO	YES / NO	YES / NO	
History	YES / NO	YES / NO	YES / NO	YES / NO	
English	YES / NO	YES / NO	YES / NO	YES / NO	
Biology	YES / NO	YES / NO	YES / NO	YES / NO	
German	YES / NO	YES / NO	YES / NO	YES / NO	
Choir	YES / NO	YES / NO	YES / NO	YES / NO	

Note to teacher: Please circle Yes or No in each box, list comments and sign. Thanks!

🏋️ *Chapter Summary/Preview of Chapter 3* 🏋️

Congratulations **on finishing a very important chapter on the "nuts and bolts" of behavior change. You should now have a pretty good understanding of a number of very valuable tools that may be used with your child, including:**

- Ways to prevent problems before they start

- Ways to change behaviors through using *Clear Requests*

- Targeting *Behavior Goals* by using Tracking Forms and Point Charts

- The nuts and bolts of building a Point Chart to use with your child

- *Linking* rewards and consequences to daily Point Chart goals

These behavior change tools represent only part of the puzzle. Chapter 3 focuses on the discipline tools you will need to help your child become as successful as possible.

Chapter 3 Will Focus on the Following Tools:

💡 **Rules and discipline techniques that really work!**
   -"Time out"
   -Privilege removal
   -Work chores

💡 **Barriers to effective discipline: Reasons we fail as parents.**

This page left blank for note taking.

CHAPTER 3

Setting Limits: Tools for Building an Effective Discipline Plan for Children with ADD/ADHD

48

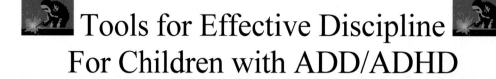

Tools for Effective Discipline
For Children with ADD/ADHD

Introduction

In the last chapter we learned the "nuts and bolts" of developing contracts and Point Charts to use as teaching tools. This chapter focuses on the next set of important teaching tools: Discipline and Limit Setting.

One of the ways that kids learn is by *testing* or *pushing their limits*. All children need to know where their limits are. They learn their limits when they are exposed to *Effective Discipline* and when parents and caregivers use healthy and effective *Limit Setting* tools. This is especially important for kids with ADD/ADHD who typically struggle with *SHOOTING FROM THE HIP, PUTTING ON THE BRAKES and MISSING THE IMPORTANT THINGS.*

Discipline and Limit Setting tools need to be healthy and firm. However, this *does not mean* they need to be harsh or painful. Harsh and painful discipline techniques usually cause more problems than they solve. The tools provided in this chapter have been proven to work, and to work without being harsh or causing pain. In fact, these tools have been used with great success with teenage felons, so we are certain they will work well with your child!

Let's go on to the next page to view our Road Map  to Chapter 3.

ROAD MAP TO CHAPTER 3

THINGS WE ARE GOING TO COVER IN THIS CHAPTER

You are about to begin a very important chapter on the *Tools for Building an Effective Discipline Plan for Kids with ADD/ADHD*. The areas we will cover are listed below:

- Breaking Through the *Barriers to Effective and Healthy Discipline*
- The "4 Fs" of *Effective and Healthy Discipline*
- Using *Clear and Consistent Rules*
- The Use of *Time Out*
- Using *Work Chores*
- Using *Privilege Removal*
- Combining Point Charts and *Effective/Healthy Discipline*

Tools for Effective Discipline for Children With ADD/ADHD

Please make sure you have read Chapter 1 (*ADD/ADHD Explained*) and Chapter 2 (*The Nuts and Bolts of Behavior Management: Teaching New Behaviors to Kids With ADD/ADHD*) before going on to read about the discipline tools described in the rest of this chapter. Make sure you understand what ADD/ADHD is, and how to teach children who struggle with *SHOOTING FROM THE HIP, PUTTING ON THE BRAKES* and *MISSING THE IMPORTANT THINGS* before you attempt to apply the Discipline/Limit Setting tools in this chapter.

Applying the tools in Chapter 3 before reading the first two chapters in this manual may end up causing you and your child more problems than it solves. Remember, kids who struggle with ADD/ADHD really need to *hear about the good things* they do about *5 times more often* than they hear about their mistakes! *5 TIMES MORE OFTEN*!

If you haven't read the first two chapters, please go back and review them before going on to the next page. If you have read them, go on to the following pages to learn about:

> ➢ Breaking Through the *Barriers to Effective and Healthy Discipline*

> ➢ The *"4 Fs" of Effective and Healthy Discipline*

> ➢ Using *Clear and Consistent Rules*

> ➢ The Use of *Time Out*

> ➢ Using *Work Chores*

> ➢ Using *Privilege Removal*

> ➢ Combining *Point Charts* and *Effective/Healthy Discipline*

BREAKING THROUGH THE BARRIERS TO EFFECTIVE AND HEALTHY DISCIPLINE

Raising kids using Effective and Healthy Discipline techniques like the ones you will learn in this manual can be very difficult. Discipline and Limit Setting for children with ADD/ADHD who are struggling with *SHOOTING FROM THE HIP, PUTTING ON THE BRAKES* and *MISSING THE IMPORTANT THINGS* can be truly challenging.

The more common barriers to Effective and Healthy Discipline are listed in the table below. These barriers and the steps to breaking through them are described on the next few pages.

The 6 Barriers to Effective and Healthy Discipline

1. Not disciplining until becoming "really mad"
2. Giving more than one consequence
3. Overreacting or not knowing what to do
4. Threatening discipline
5. Not following through
6. Adults in the home disagreeing about discipline

Please turn the page to read about some things you may be able to do to deal with these difficulties when you encounter them.

Breaking Through the Barriers to Effective and Healthy Discipline

Parenting and teaching children with ADD/ADHD has been likened to being pecked to death by ducks. No single peck is a big deal – rather, it's the seemingly relentless and never-ending nature of the problem that is often the cause of the stress, anxiety, frustration, fear and anger parents and caregivers often feel. The stress of parenting and teaching kids with ADD/ADHD usually can be lessened by understanding and managing the barriers to Effective and Healthy Discipline. These are described below:

The 6 Barriers to Effective and Healthy Discipline

1. Not disciplining until becoming "really mad:" This often happens when we wait too long before setting a limit or disciplining. One example of this could be the feelings parents experience when having to repeatedly tell a child to do something in order for the child to respond. The best way to prevent this is to set a limit when the behavior is small or after we have made the same request twice. The *Clear Requests* procedure we learned in Chapter 2 can really help with this.

   Getting really angry in situations where you have to set limits on kids can often be a sign that *your* stress levels are getting really high. Some important tools for managing your stress are covered in Chapter 5.

The 6 Barriers to
Effective and Healthy Discipline
 (Continued)

2. <u>Giving more than one consequence</u>: **This often happens when we are really frustrated, tired, stressed or angry. It is important to remember that the goal of Limit Setting and** *Effective and Healthy Discipline* **is to teach – not to "make them pay."**

   If you are frequently giving more than one consequence when your kid is out of line, you may be struggling with feelings of hopelessness or high levels of family stress. As we mentioned above, some very helpful tools for managing your stress level are covered in Chapter 5.

3. <u>Overreacting or not knowing what to do</u>: **This situation can result when we don't have a Limit Setting/Discipline plan. The best way to prevent such problems is to develop an** *Effective and Healthy Discipline* **plan to be used at home and at school with your child. The plan should take advantage of the tools taught on later pages (Time Out, Work Chores, Privilege Removal), and should be agreed upon by all significant adults working with your child (such as parents and teachers). This plan should also be linked to the Point Chart you are using with your child, as outlined in Chapter 2.**

   Once you have formed your plan, write it down and keep it handy! If you don't have a plan or can't find it when you need it, trying to think one up in the heat of the moment can be very stressful and probably won't work very well.

   If after reading the rest of this chapter you are still having difficulty developing an *Effective and Healthy Discipline* **plan to use with your child with ADD/ADHD, then we recommend you get some help from a psychologist or other behavioral professional to build one.**

The 6 Barriers to
Effective and Healthy Discipline

 (Continued)

4. <u>Threatening discipline:</u> **If you are simply threatening to set limits, one of two things may be happening. First, you may be too busy to enforce the limits or to be consistent. This often happens when life is going too fast. Remember to take the time you need to teach! Second, your kids may have learned "how far they can go" before they have to do what you have told them to do. We all have patterns, and our children learn ours – even the patterns we don't know we have!**

5. <u>Not following through:</u> **Failing to follow through is one of the most dangerous and difficult of the *Barriers to Healthy and Effective Discipline*. It can accidentally teach any number of unhealthy behaviors. When we fail to set a limit, we reward unhealthy behaviors such as noncompliance or whining without intending to do so. If we fail to follow through somewhat randomly, the kids are occasionally getting a payoff for unhealthy behaviors (things like not minding). When the payoff is somewhat random, kids will lock into a "Maybe this time I will get away with it if I just hold out" mode of behavior. This is a very powerful mode and one that is very difficult to get people to break. It is also the main reason that people pump so much money into slot machines at casinos – the payoff is somewhat random, so the person keeps putting quarters into the machine because they are hoping for the payoff each time they pull the lever!**

Not following through usually happens when we are tired, distracted, frustrated or angry. The best remedy for this is to take care of yourself and to manage your stress effectively. It is also important to remember that no one is completely consistent in their follow-through with Limit Setting and/or Discipline. Total, 100 percent follow-through is an ideal goal to set for yourself. However, if you follow through 85 percent of the time, count yourself a winner!

The 6 Barriers to
Effective and Healthy Discipline

 (Continued)

6. <u>Adults in the home disagreeing about discipline</u>: **As we mentioned above, having all adults in the home "on the same page" is very important to achieving** *Effective and Healthy Discipline*. **When the adults don't agree, life in the family home can be stressful and unpredictable. Open communication between all adults in the home and the use of effective negotiating skills makes** *Effective and Healthy Discipline* **natural and easy.**

We know that complete agreement among all the adults in your home is not possible: Disagreements are a natural part of life. However, it is essential that all adults in the home support each other when setting limits and avoid disagreement in front of their kids (as long as the limits are not neglectful or abusive). When disagreements happen, work them out in private – not in front of your kids!

Now that we have covered the *Barriers to Effective and Healthy Discipline*, **the remainder of this chapter will discuss the following** *Effective and Healthy Discipline* **tools:**

> ➢ The *"4 Fs"* of *Effective and Healthy Discipline*

> ➢ Using *Clear and Consistent Rules*

> ➢ The Use of *Time Out*

> ➢ Using *Work Chores*

> ➢ Using *Privilege Removal*

> ➢ Combining *Point Charts* and *Effective/Healthy Discipline*

The Keys to Effective and Healthy Discipline

When kids need discipline, we need to have an entire toolbox of *Effective and Healthy Discipline* **tools at our fingertips. These tools need to be easy to use and used consistently when teaching our children how to be happy and successful people. Our discipline tools need to follow the** *"4 Fs"* **of** *Effective and Healthy Discipline.* **Our tools must be:**

- *Firm:* Discipline tools need to be clear and ***should not be "soft peddled"*** in the attempt to be nice. Remember, we are trying to build a connection between behaviors and consequences. We do not want to be vague or unclear when dealing with our children – we want them to notice us and to learn the lesson.

- *Fair:* We should always ***"make the punishment fit the crime."*** In other words, if the infraction is small, the punishment should be small. Remember that we are not trying to inflict pain, nor are we "trying to make them pay." Rather we are simply attempting to teach.

- *Friendly:* Avoid yelling and negative tones. Try to keep your voice calm. Remember, kids will match your tones – if you come at them in an angry way, they will probably respond in the same manner. Always remember your goal is to teach, not to "vent" on the kid who needs discipline.

- *Frequent:* Remember that discipline is an important teaching tool, and we need to discipline every single time our child misbehaves. Inconsistent discipline can be confusing and can cause more problems than it solves. The goal of discipline is to teach – not confuse!

USING CLEAR AND CONSISTENT RULES

The first step to using healthy discipline is to provide *Clear and Consistent Rules.* When *Clear and Consistent Rules* are agreed on by all adults in the home and are explained to kids in ways they will understand, everyone in the home will be happier, healthier and more successful!

Clear and Consistent Rules make life predictable, comfortable and safe. Unclear and confusing rules make life stressful and unpredictable, and can make your home life harder than it has to be!

Take a minute and think about the rules in your home. Then list them on the lines below.

House Rules

1. _____

2. _____

3. _____

4. _____

5. _____

Please go on to the next page.

CLEAR AND CONSISTENT RULES – PART 2

Please take a moment and think about the rules you listed on the last page. When we are making *Clear and Consistent Rules*, **we want to consider three important things:**

Things to Consider When Making Clear and Consistent Rules

1. Do all people in the home understand the rules?

One way to know whether or not you have *Clear Rules* is to determine if everyone in the home *understands* the rules. You might want to ask yourself if the rules are so clear that relatives visiting your home would be able to know what is expected of them if they were successfully following the rules.

2. Are the rules agreed upon by all adults in the home?

When creating *Clear Rules*, make sure all adults in the home *understand* and *agree with* the rules before trying to enforce them. If some of the adults in the home disagree with the rules, then kids will naturally take advantage of that, and perhaps be able to *divide and conquer* the adults in the home. When adults disagree about the rules, *Consistent* enforcement is very difficult and kids may easily "play" adults off one another.

3. Are the rules enforceable?

Make sure that you are able and willing to enforce a rule before you explain it to your kids. *Consistent* rule enforcement helps kids to develop the *habit* of following the rules and the *expectation* that parents and caregivers will *regularly follow through!*

Please go on to the next page.

CLEAR AND CONSISTENT RULES – PART 3

When attempting to create *Clear and Consistent Rules* **in your home, there are several pitfalls you want to avoid. Some common mistakes we make as parents are listed below.**

Common Mistakes Preventing Clear and Consistent Rules

Mistakes	Impact of Mistakes
1. The rules are not clear.	Confusion and increased stress occur when the rules are not understood by everyone in the home. Confusion creates situations that are not predictable – this is very stressful! Healthy learning depends on predictable rules! Avoid vague rules like "be good" or "be tidy" unless you define them very clearly. Point Charts are very useful ways to define tasks and rules in the home.
2. Adults disagree on the rules in the home.	As we said above, when creating *Clear and Consistent Rules*, make sure all adults in the home *understand* and *agree with* the rules before trying to enforce them. Don't allow marital problems or difficulties between the adults in the home to create more difficulties for kids with ADD/ADHD. When adults disagree with the rules, *Consistent* enforcement is very difficult. If you are an adult and disagree with a rule, it is best to discuss your concerns with the other adults in the home when the kids are not around.

Mistakes	Impact of Mistakes
3. The rules are applied differently by different adults in the home.	This often happens – even when the adults in the home don't realize it or intend for it to happen. When the rules are applied differently, kids will often *"play"* one adult off the other, or will attempt to manipulate situations to their advantage. Doing such things is natural for kids; it is also natural and necessary for adults in the home to prevent such things from happening. As we mentioned above, try to avoid letting issues or anger with other parents in the home impact the way you apply the rules for your children. Marital and relationship issues between adults need to be addressed when the kids are not around, and should never be allowed to boil over into the ways in which the rules in the home are applied. Don't try to be a "nice" parent – your children need you to be a consistent and predictable parent if they are going to be as happy and as healthy as possible.

<u>**A final thought on *Clear and Consistent Rules***</u>: The development of *Clear and Consistent Rules* will often lead to the prevention of many difficulties experienced by kids with ADD/ADHD who struggle with *SHOOTING FROM THE HIP, PUTTING ON THE BRAKES* and *MISSING THE IMPORTANT THINGS*. The use of *Clear and Consistent Rules* should also lower your overall family stress level and increase the overall success of your family.

On the following pages, we discuss some *Effective and Healthy Discipline* tools and ways to build an Effective Discipline Plan for children with ADD/ADHD.

LET'S GO TO THE NEXT PAGE TO LEARN ABOUT TIME OUT!

SOME FACTS AND MYTHS ABOUT *"TIME OUT"* - OUR FIRST HEALTHY AND EFFECTIVE DISCIPLINE TOOL

Almost everyone has heard of Time Out – we'll bet that you have. However, many people don't *really know* what Time Out is, how it works or when to use it. This section will explain those things and will hopefully do away with some of the myths about Time Out that just are not true!

What is Time Out Anyway? When kids misbehave or break the rules, they get something out of doing so – they get a reward or payoff. However, it is often very hard to figure out what the reward is in any given situation. So rather than trying to figure out what their reward is, Time Out was created to remove kids from the reward/payoff when they doing things they shouldn't. "Time Out" is actually shorthand for the expression "Time Out from reward/payoff." Let's think about an example:

> ➤ John's sister picks up one of his toys;
> ➤ John kicks his sister;
> ➤ Sister drops the toy and runs off crying.

What payoff does John get for kicking his sister? She is gone, and he has all the toys to himself – he doesn't have to share.

What happens if John is placed in Time Out for kicking his sister? He is removed from the toys he is refusing to share and is placed in a boring situation for a period of time. The payoff for kicking his sister has been removed!

SOME FACTS AND MYTHS ABOUT "TIME OUT"
(continued)

Isn't Time Out really mean? No, it is not! In fact, Time Out builds a strong link between behaviors and their consequences. If a child breaks a rule, it simply keeps him or her from receiving a payoff for doing so and can motivate them to try more appropriate ways to earn it!

Should Time Out be saved for really big problems? Absolutely not! Time Out is a small consequence and should be used when the behaviors first begin and are small. Waiting until the problem is really big before using Time Out usually doesn't work very well.

Isn't spanking better than using Time Out? In general, physical discipline techniques cause more problems than they solve. When kids are regularly spanked, the following things may happen:

1. Kids learn to *fear* their parents/caregivers rather than *respect* them.
2. Kids who are spanked regularly may become *more aggressive* and hostile with parents and caregivers.
3. Kids learn to use aggression and hitting with other kids.
4. Kids who are spanked often become angry adults.
5. Kids who are spanked are more likely to hit their spouses when they become adults.
6. Spanking often leads parents down the path to inappropriate physical discipline.

What should be done for really big problems? Work chores and the loss of privileges – things like watching TV or playing video games – are very useful effective and healthy discipline tools to use for bigger problems or as a backup to Time Out.

Let's go to the next page for the steps to using Time Out.

☆ <u>To use Time Out well, just follow these *General Guidelines*</u> ☆

1. *Select a place.*
    - ✓ **In a low traffic area**
    - ✓ **Away from everyone else in the home**

2. *Prepare the room.*
    - ✓ **"Kid-proof" the room and identify Time Out spot**

3. *Explain the procedure to the kid(s).*
    - ✓ **What "Time Out" is and how it works (see pg. 64)**

4. *Practice Time Out beforehand.*
    - ✓ **Walk through all the steps on the next page**
    - ✓ **Have all adults practice with all kids**

5. *Be consistent.*
    - ✓ **Use it regularly and well**

6. *Label the behavior that earns Time Out.*
    - ✓ **Make sure to tell kids why they are in Time Out**

7. *Don't talk to children when they're in Time Out.*
    - ✓ **Your attention may be rewarding**
    - ✓ **Kids may be mad – let them cool down**

8. *Appear calm or neutral when giving Time Out.*
    - ✓ **Remember that kids match your anger**

9. *Use a timer.*
    - ✓ **A timer lets kids know when it's over**
    - ✓ **A ticking timer reminds them time is passing**

10. *When Time Out is over, don't make children apologize.*
    - ✓ **Time-Out is like a "re-set" button**
    - ✓ **When it's over, it's time to start over!**

THE TIME OUT PROCEDURE: A STEP BY STEP GUIDE

When using Time Out as an *Effective and Healthy Discipline* tool, make sure that you follow the simple steps below. Remember for kids with ADD/ADHD, *slowing down* is very, very important!

1. LABEL THE PROBLEM: USE SIMPLE STATEMENTS:

    "Please speak to me in a polite voice."

2. WAIT 10 SECONDS, THEN WARN:

    "If you don't speak to me in a polite voice, you will go to Time Out."

3. WAIT 10 SECONDS, THEN GIVE THE CONSEQUENCE:

    "You didn't speak to me in a polite voice, so you have a 5 minute Time Out."

4. WAIT 10 SECONDS FOR CHILD TO GO:

    Remove yourself – DO NOT talk to, check on or comfort your child.

    Set the timer for 5 minutes (if 5 years old or older; otherwise 1 minute per year).

    If the child is loud, say, "Time Out begins when you are silent."

    Stay neutral: DON'T talk about the issue when time is up.

5. IF CHILD DOES NOT GO TO TIME OUT, ADD MORE MINUTES:

    Add one minute each 10 seconds until the child goes to Time Out (up to 10 minutes)

    "Okay, that's 6 minutes."
    "Okay, that's 7 minutes."

    Do not exceed 10 minutes.

 THE TIME OUT PROCEDURE: A STEP
BY STEP GUIDE (continued)

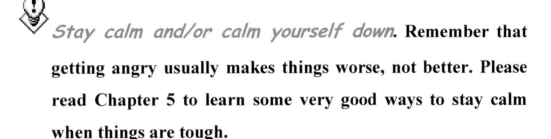 *But what if my child still won't go to Time Out?*

Testing limits and challenging authority are a natural part of growing up. Try not to be surprised when your child tests the limits and refuses to go to Time Out. When kids who struggle with *SHOOTING FROM THE HIP, PUTTING ON THE BRAKES, and MISSING THE IMPORTANT THINGS* refuse to go to Time Out, we suggest the following:

Stay calm and/or calm yourself down. **Remember that getting angry usually makes things worse, not better. Please read Chapter 5 to learn some very good ways to stay calm when things are tough.**

Have a "Back-Up Plan." **When using Time Out as a** *Effective and Healthy Discipline* **tool, having something to back it up is very important. We strongly suggest the use of Work Chores and Privilege Removal as two very good** *back-up plans.*

Let's go on to learn about Work Chores and Privilege Removal.

WORK CHORES – THE KEY TO A GOOD BACK-UP PLAN

When trying to set *Effective and Healthy Limits*, **you really want to develop a list of** *Work Chores* **to use as a** *back-up plan*. **It is very important to have this list ready, and handy,** *before* **you have a need for it! The steps to the** *Effective and Healthy* **use of** *Work Chores* **are listed below:**

- *First, try to prevent the need for Work Chores:*

  ➤ Use **Clear Requests**
  ➤ Use good timing

- *Next, make sure to follow the same command procedures used for Time Out (see previous pages).*

- *Then, if the child does not cooperate, give a Work Chore.*

- *Make sure to create chores that are:*

  ➤ Short (no more than 10-15 minutes)
  ➤ Designed to make the punishment fit the crime

- *FOLLOW THROUGH !*

  ➤ Supervise the work chore
  ➤ **Enforce** the limit by **taking away important privileges** until the Work Chore is completed

PRIVILEGE REMOVAL – BUILDING
THE LAST PART OF A GOOD BACK-UP PLAN

Privilege Removal **is a back-up plan to use when children refuse to go to Time Out and/or to do their Work Chore. Eventually, kids learn that it is easier to take small consequences (like Time Out or Work Chores) than it is to lose a privilege. The steps to** *Effective and Healthy* **use of** *Privilege Removal* **are listed below:**

- *Decide which privileges to use as back-ups. Things like:*

  - TV
  - Video Games
  - Playing With Friends

- *The privilege being taken must be under parents' control.*

  - If you can't control a privilege, don't put it on your list. If you can't control it, you probably can't take it away!

- *Remove privileges for no more than 1 to 2 hours or until Work Chore is completed.*

  - Lengthy privilege removal builds up resentment. Remember, it is the fact that the privilege is lost – not the length of time – that is important.

- *Follow Through!*

  - When you say a privilege is lost, TAKE IT that day. Keep your word.
  - Remove the privilege ASAP!
  - The sooner the discipline event is over, the easier it is to get on with normal, positive family life.

Combining Point Charts and Effective/Healthy Discipline – Making It All Work Together!

Remember that we are building a *system* designed to help kids who struggle with *SHOOTING FROM THE HIP, PUTTING ON THE BRAKES and MISSING THE IMPORTANT THINGS.* The best way to make sure the system you are developing is well oiled is to remember the following things:

1. *Teaching tools (like Point Charts) need to mesh together with Effective and Healthy Discipline tools (like Time Out and Work Chores) like the cogs of a well-oiled machine.*

2. *Discipline only teaches kids what NOT to do. Teaching tools like Point Charts and School Cards teach kids what we want them to do!*

3. *Include your kid's teacher in the process: Try to use the same rules at school and at home. The more things are the same, the better they will work! More on this in later chapters!*

4. *Effective discipline gives kids what they need, which is not always the same thing as giving them what they want.*
   Remember the old story about the bird in the cow pie:

   > *A mother bird left her baby in the nest while she went out to hunt for worms.*
   >
   > *The baby bird was playing around the edge of the nest and fell out.*
   >
   > *The bird's wings were weak, and he could not fly back up into the tree. So he cried and cried, "Help me! I'm going to freeze to death!"*

   (continued on the next page)

Along came a cow. She couldn't pick him up and return him to the tree, so she did the only thing she could do for him – she dropped a cow pie on him to keep him warm.

But now the bird was unhappy. He cried and cried, "Help me, help me! I have just been dumped on and I am all messy and smelly!"

Along came a coyote, who pulled the bird out of the cow pie, took him down to the creek and bathed him. He dried the bird off and got him all warm and snuggly. The coyote then gave him a big smile and ATE HIM!

The moral of the story: The people who dump on you are not necessarily your enemies, and the ones who pull you out are not necessarily your friends!

- **If you remember these things, you will be well on your way to building a well-oiled behavior management plan that will help your kids succeed. Successful kids certainly make life less stressful and more enjoyable for their parents and their families!**

Let's go on to the next page for a summary and a preview of the next chapter: *Helping Kids With ADD/ADHD Get Organized and Make Friends.*

70

Chapter Summary/Preview of Chapter 4

Congratulations on finishing a very important chapter on the *Tools for Building an Effective Discipline Plan* for children with ADD/ADHD. You should now have a pretty good understanding of a number of very important tools that may be used with your child, including:

- Breaking Through the *Barriers to Effective and Healthy Discipline*

- The *"4 Fs"* of Effective and Healthy Discipline

- Using *Clear and Consistent Rules*

- The Use of *Time Out*

- Using *Work Chores*

- Using *Privilege Removal*

- Combining *Point Charts* and *Effective/Healthy Discipline*

These tools for changing behavior are *only one part of the puzzle*. Be sure to combine them with the skills you learned in earlier chapters, as well as the skills you will learn in the last three chapters of this manual. The remaining chapters are:

Chapter 4: *Helping Kids With ADD/ADHD Get Organized and Make Friends*

Chapter 5 *What to Do When the Kids Are Driving You Nuts: Stress Management for Parents*

Chapter 6: *Involvement and Communication: Two Antidotes for Low Self-Esteem*

This page left blank for note taking.

CHAPTER 4
Helping Kids With ADD/ADHD
Get Organized and Make Friends

Helping Kids With ADD/ADHD Get Organized and Make Friends

Introduction

We have covered a lot of information so far in this manual. We presented an understanding what ADD/ADHD is and what it isn't, provided useful teaching tools and offered healthy discipline techniques. This chapter stresses the ways you can have a positive impact on your child with ADD/ADHD by helping her or him develop good organizational skills and useful social skills. These are two very important areas for kids who typically struggle with *SHOOTING FROM THE HIP, PUTTING ON THE BRAKES and MISSING THE IMPORTANT THINGS.*

We hope you will find the tools in this chapter to be useful. Children who are organized and are good at making and keeping friends tend to be happier and healthier. In addition, families with children who are organized and socially successful tend to be less stressed out and often appear to be happier as well.

Let's go on to the next page to view our Road Map to Chapter 4!

ROAD MAP TO CHAPTER 4

THINGS WE ARE GOING TO COVER IN THIS CHAPTER

You are about to begin a vitally important chapter on ways that good organizational and social skills can lead to good self-esteem, self-confidence and school success. The areas we will cover are listed below:

- *Getting Kids With ADD/ADHD Organized – An Important Place to Start*

- *21 Specific Ways to Help Kids With ADD/ADHD Get Organized*

- *Making and Keeping Friends*

- *Mastering the 9 Friendship Challenges*

These key areas should prove very useful to your kids as they try to navigate through life in happy and healthy ways.

☺ Let's get started! ☺

Getting Kids with ADD/ADHD Organized – An Important Place to Start

When it comes to organization and neatness, kids are all different. Some are naturally good at it and some find it a daily struggle. Those with ADD/ADHD who struggle with *SHOOTING FROM THE HIP, PUTTING ON THE BRAKES, and MISSING THE IMPORTANT THINGS* often find neatness and organization more difficult than other kids.

This section of our book focuses on ways parents and other adults can help kids with ADD/ADHD be more organized in their approach to school, homework and their home lives. Kids who feel more successful at running their own lives generally do better and feel more self-confident. Additionally, we offer 9 ways you can help your child with ADD/ADHD make and keep friends.

Over the years we have found the 21 suggestions listed on the next several pages to be very useful to parents trying to help kids who struggle with ADD/ADHD. They are taken from current scientific literature and the experiences of the clinical staff at Dr. Al's clinic (Parmelee and Winebarger Psychological Consulting). Some of the suggestions won't be right for you, but we ask that you look them over and try the ones you think might be useful in your home and with your child. Here they are!

21 Ways to Help Kids With ADD/ADHD
Get Organized

1. Create and write down a schedule. This should be clear and easily understood. It is often most useful if you and your child create the schedule together. This will increase understanding and investment in the process. It is also important to post the schedule where it can be seen easily by you and your child.

2. Use a Daily School Report Card. We are big fans of this idea, and have found such cards to work very well. You can create a simple half-page form that can be completed each day by your child's teacher. This form will give you feedback about how your child did at school that day. It should have a place for the child to write in homework assignments, and a place for the teacher to let you know if any assignments are overdue. This Daily School Report Card system gives you and your child nearly immediate feedback every day. When we let days or weeks go by without this type of school communication, very valuable time can be lost. Remember the old expression, "You can't un-ring the bell."

3. Create a useful way for your child to carry papers around at school and between school and home. Given that you know your child very well, sit down with him or her and develop a notebook/backpack system. Some kids work better with:

   ➢ A separate notebook for each subject;
   ➢ A large notebook with different pockets for each subject;
   ➢ Accordion files.

   Simply try out different systems until you find the one that works best for your child.

(Continued)

4. **Create a good space for your child to do homework.** Make sure you remove distracting things (like TV) and that the homework spot is not in a high-traffic area. Stock the homework place with all the tools necessary to do the work and keep it stocked throughout the school year. You wouldn't ask a carpenter to build without making sure all the tools were available, would you?

5. **Have extra supplies.** Try not to rely on your child to bring home all the pencils and notebook papers he or she may need. Avoid the stress of having to "hunt up" supplies when your child sits down to do homework. Remember that an ounce of prevention is worth a pound of cure!

6. **Create a regular time for homework.** We are also big fans of what we call Read and Study Time. This is a time when the child goes to the homework location each day and sits and does homework. If no homework has been assigned that day, the child simply reads. This creates a structured routine and will remove much of the motivation for trying to get out of doing homework. We usually include this in our Point Charts, as you can see in the example Point Chart in Chapter 2.

7. **Create a filing system.** Kids with ADD/ADHD often appear to be lost in a sea of clutter! Create places for kids to put papers and supplies when they are no longer needed. Some parents suggest giving kids their own small filing cabinet to use when creating a filing system. Small plastic filing boxes can also be a colorful and useful approach: Try using different colors for different subjects and/or different projects.

21 Ways to Help Kids With ADD/ADHD
Get Organized

(Continued)

8. **Pack everything away when homework is complete.** Have the child put all supplies away and place all items needed for the next school day in the backpack or book bag. This will help your child to avoid the pitfalls of procrastination – like completing homework only to forget to take it to school and turn it in!

9. **Label things.** Have your child get into the habit of labeling papers and homework assignments (with the date and subject). This will be very helpful when you and your child are trying to sort and file!

10. **Create a homework log.** This could be a simple list of assignments, their due dates, and a place for the child, teacher and parent to sign off after the homework is completed/turned in. This will help kids, parents and teachers keep in touch on a daily basis, and help prevent unpleasant surprises (like overdue projects)!

11. **Break large projects down into a series of small projects – and schedule them!** Large projects often present serious minefields for kids with ADD/ADHD. Breaking projects down into smaller, "doable" subparts will prove very helpful to your child and should reduce the frustration of an overwhelming project.

12. **When you are helping your child, or giving your child directions, have her or him repeat them to you to make sure they understand.** Kids often nod when adults pause in their talking, or say "OK" when we stop talking even when they have not processed everything we have said. Having kids repeat the instructions ensures that they know what is expected of them.

21 Ways to Help Kids With ADD/ADHD Get Organized

(Continued)

13. **Check the teacher's Web site.** Many teachers today have their own Web sites where they list things like homework and due dates. These can be very useful to review regularly with your child. Log in and read the Web site with your child and together update schedules, projects and files as needed. One of the best teacher sites around is run by a 5th grade teacher in Dr. Al's local area. Check it out at www.learningforkids.com.

14. **Call the homework hotline.** Many schools have homework hotlines where parents can hear a recording about the assignments and projects of the day. If your school has one, call it with your child each and every day.

15. **Use graphic organizers.** These can be simple things such as timelines, project maps, checklists and decision trees (diagrams). Create these with your child and agree on their meaning and their uses. Such aids allow kids to map their thoughts and to visually see the upcoming assignments.

16. **Have your child organize their files on a computer.** The computer can be a very useful organizational tool if used correctly. Help your child develop a system for keeping track of projects and related computer files.

17. **Use visual prompts.** Post noticeable reminders in key places like your child's desk or school locker. Placing them on the refrigerator door can be helpful to you as well as your child. Use displays like banners, charts or colorful pie graphs. Change the form of the reminders to keep them interesting. Put pictures on the outsides of notebooks to show what the subject is.

(Continued)

18. **Use Point Charts to target behavioral goals.** We discussed these in some detail in Chapter 2. Remember a very good way to prompt a child to be organized is to remind him or her to "Go check your Point Chart!"

19. **Encourage the use of alternative tools.** This could be something as simple as having your child explore using a computer to type assignments rather than writing everything by hand. Kids with ADD/ADHD often have terrible handwriting and feel very frustrated when their hands cannot keep up with their thoughts! Allow older students to take notes at school with a laptop, or to record teachers with a microcassette recorder.

20. **Develop time management strategies.** Time management is a very difficult task for kids with ADD/ADHD. Encourage the use of such tools as watches or timers. Many watches have vibrating alarms that can be used throughout the day in ways that won't disturb others.

21. **Encourage and praise your child for their efforts!** Remember to encourage them for trying – even when they fail. We are all works in progress and we want to instill in kids the motivation to continue to try even when things are difficult!

Once you have reviewed these suggestions, think about the ones that might work best for your child and give them a try. Then please move on to the next section focused on the *tools needed for making and keeping friends.*

Please turn the page!

Making and Keeping Friends

Kids with ADD/ADHD who struggle with *SHOOTING FROM THE HIP, PUTTING ON THE BRAKES* and *MISSING THE IMPORTANT THINGS* often have a lot of trouble making and keeping friends. This is so true that many researchers have been able to go into schools and figure out which kids are likely to have ADD/ADHD just by having other kids identify classmates who struggle with making and keeping friends.

Why do kids with ADD/ADHD have so much trouble learning how to make and keep friendships? Remember that one of the things kids with ADD/ADHD often struggle with is *Missing the Important Things*. One of the ways we learn how to make and keep friends is by paying attention to the feedback we receive from them and from the world around us. Unfortunately, much of the feedback isn't very noticeable, and is often missed by kids with ADD/ADHD. Consider the following scene:

1. *Impulsive Al:* Ten-year-old Impulsive Al wants to talk to a new kid, so he runs up to the kid, gets right in his face, and says, "Hey man, wanna play?"

2. *New Kid:* The New Kid feels that Al is standing way too close to him, so he backs up a little. Given that Al has trouble with *Missing the Important Things*, he doesn't realize that the New Kid is trying to create a comfortable distance between them.

3. *Impulsive Al:* Al gets back in the New Kid's face and says, "Do you wanna play or what?" in an annoyed tone.

4. *New Kid:* The New Kid says, "Get away from me, man!" He then shoves past Impulsive Al who ends up feeling rejected and sad. Al doesn't understand that he was coming on way too strong. He believes he was simply trying to talk to the New Kid. He doesn't get it because *he didn't notice the feedback!*

Making and Keeping Friends
(continued)

In situations like the one on the last page, kids with ADD/ADHD who struggle with *MISSING THE IMPORTANT THINGS* are cheated out of many of the social lessons that we all need to learn if we are going to be successful when making and keeping friends. This problem can be even more complicated for kids who also struggle with *SHOOTING FROM THE HIP* and *PUTTING ON THE BRAKES*. These kids can become frustrated and may often try more and more harmful things that get them into more and more trouble with their peers. As a result, kids with ADD/ADHD often end up feeling that no one likes them, and that no one wants to be their friend. These kids often end up with very little self-confidence and very low self-esteem. Their social life can become a barren and lonely wasteland.

What can parents and teachers do about this? The next couple of pages list 9 of the most difficult challenges kids with ADD/ADHD face when trying to make and keep friends. After each challenge we have listed several *Skills for Meeting the Challenge* that you can teach to your child. Remember that parents are the most important teachers kids will ever have, so use your wisdom, experience and knowledge to help your child learn each of the skills listed. If you feel that you cannot teach these skills, or you need more information, consult your local school psychologist, clinical psychologist or your child's teacher to get some help. Our company will be releasing our Social Skills Toolbox within the next year, so keep an eye out for it!

84

 It's Time to Master the 9 Friendship Challenges!

CHALLENGE #1: *MAKING FRIENDS: MEETING SOMEONE (1 ON 1) AND STARTING A CONVERSATION OR ACTIVITY*

Many children with ADHD have a difficult time in new social situations because they start off on the wrong foot. They may be overly aggressive or they may not give clear messages about their intentions. Once they have been perceived by others as lacking skills in this area, they are much more likely to be rejected, excluded, or treated in other negative ways. Basically, if things start off badly, they are likely to continue downhill. This is true in terms of the ways adults and other children will interact kids with ADD/ADHD. Below are some things you can focus on when trying to help your child with ADD/ADHD master this challenge:

Skills for Meeting This Challenge

1. **Maintain eye contact.**

2. **Approach the other person at a reasonable speed (not too fast or too slow).**

3. **Wait for a pause or other appropriate time to begin speaking.**

4. **Learn appropriate initial or introductory statements (like saying "Hello," followed by a pause to let the other person respond).**

5. **Learn additional conversational skills if you want to just keep talking (like finding common things to talk about).**

6. **Learn how to invite the other person to do an activity.**

7. **Learn how to join in an activity that the other person is doing.**

CHALLENGE #2: HELPING EACH OTHER: COOPERATION WITH PEERS

Because many children with ADD/ADHD have difficulty staying focused on activities, and because they are often rejected by peers they may lack a clear sense of what it means to cooperate with others. They may tend to either do things on their own or not at all. Cooperation skills allow children to work as a team to accomplish common goals. When children are working toward common goals, they tend get along better and are more accepting of each other. By teaching children these skills, you can help them to identify when a situation calls for cooperation and to know what to do when it comes to working with their peers. Here are some things you can focus on when attempting to help your child with ADD/ADHD master this challenge:

Skills for Meeting This Challenge

1. Learn to tell the difference between times for working together with friends and when working together wouldn't be the best thing to do.

2. Learn to agree with friends about what the goal is.

3. Learn how to develop a plan for really good and healthy ways to work together with friends.

4. Learn to assign jobs or roles to people.

Please turn the page!

Time to Master the Friendship Challenges
(continued)

CHALLENGE #3: FITTING IN: RESPONDING TO CLOSED GROUPS

Entering a group of children who are already interacting can be difficult. If the timing isn't right or an overly aggressive approach is used, the child is likely to be excluded. On the other hand, many children simply avoid situations in which groups are already playing together because they fear they may feel disliked or need to wait for an invitation. Teaching kids the skills listed below will help your children learn to take the initiative in ways that are likely to bring about positive outcomes. Children who learn good group entry skills are likely to experience improvements in many other areas, including peer acceptance, adult acceptance and self-esteem. Some things you can focus on when attempting to help your child with ADD/ADHD master this challenge are listed below:

Skills for Meeting This Challenge

1. Think about healthy ways to approach groups, like:

   - How fast you approach the group;
   - How close you come to the group before stopping to talk.

2. Identify the right time for speaking up.

3. Have ideas in place about what to say when you want to enter a group.

4. Dealing with rejection – what to do when the group won't let you join.

Please turn the page!

CHALLENGE #4: *SAYING HOW YOU FEEL AND UNDERSTANDING HOW OTHERS FEEL*

It is common for children with ADD/ADHD to act out feelings rather than using words to say how they feel. For instance, rather than saying "I feel really mad right now," a child with ADD/ADHD is more likely to have a temper tantrum. Identifying feelings can be helpful because a child can learn to use words as an alternative to action as a way to express feelings. Also, it can help a child to learn that there are more feelings than just *good* and *bad*: Some of the feelings associated with *bad*, for instance, can be sad, confused, frustrated, tired, sick or angry. By learning to tell the difference, a child may begin to develop different ways of dealing with different feelings. Finally, saying how you feel and understanding how others feel can be important in communicating with others. Below we list some things you can focus on when attempting to help your child with ADD/ADHD master this challenge:

Skills for Meeting This Challenge

1. **Identify a range of feelings.**

2. **Learn ways to figure out what you are feeling.**

3. **Learn ways to figure out what someone else is feeling.**

4. **Describe times when you experience the feelings.**

5. **Learn ways to tell others what your feelings are.**

Please turn the page!

88

CHALLENGE #5: *SOLVING A PROBLEM*

Many children with ADD/ADHD begin to believe that the problems they have with their friends and peers are unsolvable. When a problem arises, the choices they make are very limited in nature and often have the result of making the problem bigger. They have difficulty walking away from problems or "disengaging." They rarely have the skills for problem solving. Unfortunately, problems are bound to arise in the day-to-day lives of children. Therefore, a lack of skills in this area can pose a major problem. When children are able to solve problems through compromise or by considering a variety of solutions, they feel much more confident about dealing with daily hassles and are generally able to develop closer relationships with peers and adults. Here are some things you can focus on when attempting to help your child with ADD/ADHD master this challenge:

Skills for Meeting This Challenge

1. Help your child identify what causes fights between children or between children and grown-ups.

2. When fights happen, discuss with your child things that make the problem bigger.

3. When fights happen, discuss with your child things that make the problem smaller.

4. Practice solving common problems, such as when two people want to play with the same toy.

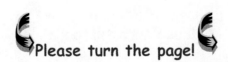
Please turn the page!

Time to Master the Friendship Challenges
(continued)

CHALLENGE #6: *KEEPING FRIENDS*

This challenge is directly related to Challenge #1, *Making Friends: Meeting Someone (1 on 1) and Starting a Conversation or Activity*. Once kids with ADD/ADHD learn to make friends, they then need to learn ways to take care of the relationships they form. Often the feedback about what we are doing in social situations is very subtle, and kids who struggle with *SHOOTING FROM THE HIP, PUTTING ON THE BRAKES* and *MISSING THE IMPORTANT THINGS* miss many of the subtle social skills lessons being taught in their environments (like the playground). Below we list some things you can focus on when attempting to help your child with ADD/ADHD master this challenge:

Skills for Meeting This Challenge

1. Smile! It makes people want to walk with you for a mile.

2. Share! It makes you easy to bare.

3. Be a buddy! It makes bullies melt like putty.

4. Be a great sport! Then others won't think you're just a snort.

5. Be upfront and confront! Because tattling is rattling.

6. Ask like an adult! Because whining makes people want to push you away.

Please turn the page!

90

CHALLENGE #7: *HANDLING ANGER*

While we have already talked about emotions in general, this challenge deals specifically with anger. Kids with ADD/ADHD often struggle with anger and frustration they experience from the difficulties that develop in their lives as a result of *SHOOTING FROM THE HIP, PUTTING ON THE BRAKES* and *MISSING THE IMPORTANT THINGS.* **Help your child focus on the skills needed to handle the angry feelings they experience when they are rejected. Parents should attempt to help their kids realize that anger is a secondary emotion that is always brought on by a more vulnerable feeling. Below we list some specific ways that children can defuse their anger in a way that doesn't destroy anything or hurt someone else.**

Skills for Meeting This Challenge

1. Know the anger rule: "Break nothing and hurt no one."

2. Make sure you know why you are angry.

3. Know that anger is normal.

4. Find healthy ways to express your anger – ways that are helpful and not hurtful.

5. Learn how to use "A Bug and a Wish" statements ("It *bugs* me when you do that and I *wish* that you would stop.")

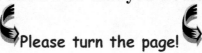
Please turn the page!

Time to Master the Friendship Challenges
(continued)

CHALLENGE #8: *GIVE YOURSELF A BREAK*

Earlier challenges listed the importance of helping kids with ADD/ADHD recognize their own feelings and the feelings of others. Once kids with ADD/ADHD begin to develop the skills to recognize negative thoughts and feelings, they need good tools to manage those feelings and to keep from becoming overwhelmed. Kids who are feeling this way often make poor choices on how to handle their feelings. So we want to introduce them to a new method for dealing with being overwhelmed. We call these relaxation techniques. We want them to think about ways in which they can learn to calm themselves down so that they can think through situations and make good choices when they feel overwhelmed. Below we list some things you can focus on when attempting to help your child with ADD/ADHD master this challenge:

Skills for Meeting This Challenge

1. Identify ways to calm yourself down.

2. Learn to step back and take a few deep breaths.

3. Parents should become familiar with the stress management tools presented in *Chapter 5: What to Do When the Kids Are Driving You Nuts: Stress Management for Parents*. Once you begin to practice these things, you can teach them to your child with ADD/ADHD.

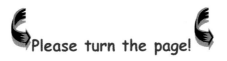
Please turn the page!

Time to Master the Friendship Challenges
(continued)

CHALLENGE #9: *ACCEPT IMPERFECTION*

A difficult dilemma that often confronts children with ADD/ADHD is feeling they are not "good enough." They feel like they are always making mistakes and they lose confidence in themselves. At the root of this feeling is the self-imposed expectation that they have to be perfect. This leads to a great deal of frustration and disappointment with themselves. Often this interferes with their ability to participate productively in the problem solving process. It is often difficult for kids with ADD/ADHD to accept imperfection. We want to encourage kids to accept the fact that everyone makes mistakes. We also want to give them ways to cope with the disappointment of having made a mistake. Instead of beating themselves up emotionally, we want them to learn to focus on their successes. In other words, we want them to learn to compliment themselves and accept compliments from others. Below are some things you can focus on when attempting to help your child with ADD/ADHD master this challenge:

Skills for Meeting This Challenge

1. Understand that everyone makes mistakes.

2. Learn to compliment yourself.

3. Learn to accept compliments from others.

If after reading this section on *Making and Keeping Friends* you need more information or guidance, please contact a local mental health provider or the professionals at your school for help. Schools often run social skills or "friendship" groups and are often looking for new members. Also, as we mentioned earlier, our company will be releasing our Social Skills Toolbox within the next year, so be sure to look for it!

Chapter Summary/Preview of Chapter 5

Congratulations **on finishing a very important chapter on** *Helping Kids With ADD/ADHD Get Organized and Make Friends.* **We hope you have found it helpful, and that you will be able to successfully use the ideas we have listed there. If you are struggling with understanding or using any of the ideas presented here, we urge you to contact a local psychologist, school psychologist or other mental health professional for assistance. After reading through the previous pages we hope you now have a pretty good understanding of the following areas:**

- *Getting Kids with ADD/ADHD Organized – An Important Place to Start*
- *21 Ways to Help Kids With ADD/ADHD Get Organized*
- *Making and Keeping Friends*
- *Mastering the 9 Friendship Challenges*

Please continue on to Chapter 5: *What To Do When The Kids Are Driving You Nuts: Stress Management For Parents*

<u>**Chapter 5 Will Focus on the Following Tools:**</u>
- *Understanding* stress
- *Recognizing* stress
- *Managing* Stress

CHAPTER 5
What to Do When the Kids Are Driving You Nuts: Stress Management for Parents

What to Do When the Kids Are Driving You Nuts: Stress Management for Parents

Introduction

In the last several chapters we have covered a number of really important topics for parents of kids who struggle with ADD/ADHD. We have defined ADD/ADHD and discussed how to assess those difficulties (Chapter 1). We have discussed effective ways to teach (Chapter 2), and effective limit setting/discipline techniques (Chapter 3). However, we realize that parents will not be able to use all these good tools if they are feeling stressed out! We understand that parenting is hard – especially when families are struggling with trying to help kids with ADD/ADHD manage their difficulties with *SHOOTING FROM THE HIP, PUTTING ON THE BRAKES* and *MISSING THE IMPORTANT THINGS*.

In Chapter 3 we mentioned the old expression about how hard parenting can be:

> Parenting is like being pecked to death by ducks….
> No single peck is a big deal…
> Rather it's the relentless, never ending quality of the job!

This chapter will help you understand the stress you feel and will teach you some new tools to manage that stress. We realize that this chapter is very brief, but we hope it will be useful to you as you parent your children because you are their most important resource. We also realize we need to take care of you and that you need to take care of yourself in order to be a successful parent to your child with ADD/ADHD.

Let's go on to the next page to see the Road Map to *Chapter 5 – What to Do When the Kids Are Driving You Nuts: Stress Management for Parents.*

ROAD MAP TO CHAPTER 5

THINGS WE ARE GOING TO COVER IN THIS CHAPTER

You are about to begin an extremely important chapter on *What to Do When the Kids Are Driving You Nuts: Stress Management for Parents*. The areas we will cover include:

- *Understanding* stress

- *Recognizing* stress

- *Managing* Stress

  - Avoiding Unhealthy Coping Methods

  - Prevention of Stress – A Pound of Prevention

  - 7 Easy Ways to Prevent Stress

  - What You Think Really Matters

    - The Connection Between Our Minds and Bodies

    - The Connection Between Our Bodies and Minds

  - Low Cost Ways to Manage Stress

Turn the page and let's get started!

Some Ideas About Stress

This chapter will help us to *Understand Stress, Recognize Stress* and *Manage Stress*.

Goal #1: Understanding Stress

What is stress? This is a very important question. We think of stress as anything that puts a demand on you or your family. Sometimes stress comes from bad things that happen. Sometimes it comes from regular day-to-day things that happen and sometimes *it even comes from good things*! For example, you may find yourself feeling stressed out when your kids are not minding you (a bad thing), when you have to get them ready for school in the morning (a regular day-to-day thing), or when they are competing for the spelling bee championship at their school (a good thing). As you can see, stress comes from all directions. As we all know, we are never going to have a life without stress.

Stress is usually a very personal thing, and is often different for each of us. In order to better understand your own stress, try to answer the question below.

How do you know you are stressed? Take a second and think about it, then write down your ideas about *what stress is*:

_____

_____

_____

_____

Recognizing the Ways We Respond to Stress

The ways we react when we feel our boat is sinking!

Goal #2: Recognizing Stress

All of us react to stress in many different ways. In general we respond to stress with *changes in our body* (things like headaches, neck pain and stomachaches), *changes in our mood* (we may become angry or sad), and *changes in our behaviors* (we may lash out or become cranky).

Try this exercise:

Take a minute to think about the ways you respond to stress. Look at the example below and then list some examples of your own. Write down some recent situations you found stressful and then list any of the *changes in your body, changes in your mood* or *changes in your behaviors* that took place at the time.

Event	Changes in Your Body	Changes in Your Mood	Changes in Your Behaviors
(Example) Locked my keys in the car when making a quick stop at the bank.	Stomach became upset; head began to pound	Angry	Kicked the car
1.			
2.			

Please go to the next page to see a list of Early Warning Signs of Stress.

EARLY WARNING SIGNS OF STRESS:
INDICATORS OF DIFFICULTY IN COPING

This is a list of common *EARLY WARNING SIGNS OF STRESS*. Look back at your list and see if your reactions to stress are here. Remember that we all respond to stress differently.

Changes in Mood	Changes in Behavior	Changes in Body

-Not caring about things
  The "blahs"
  Recreation no longer fun
 	
-Sad
 	
-Anxiety
  Restlessness
  Agitation
  Insecurity
  Feelings of worthlessness
 	
-Irritability
  Overly sensitive
  Defensive
  Arrogant/Argumentative
  Insubordinate/Hostile
 	
-Anger
 	
-Mental Fatigue
  Preoccupied
  Difficulty concentrating
  Attentional problems
  Inflexible
 	
-Overcompensation
  Exaggerate/Grandiose
  Overworks to exhaustion
  Denies problems/symptoms
  Suspicious/Paranoid
	-Withdrawal (avoidance)
	  Social isolation
	  Work-related withdrawal
	
	-Reluctance to accept
	  responsibilities
	
	-Neglecting responsibilities
	
	-Acting out
	  Alcohol abuse
	  Gambling
	  Spending sprees
	  Promiscuity
	
	-Desperate acting out
	  Getting attention
	  Cry for help
	
	-Administrative infractions
	  Tardy to work
	  Poor appearance
	  Poor personal hygiene
	  Accident prone
	  Legal infractions
	    Indebtedness
	    Shoplifting
	    Traffic tickets
	    Fights
	    Child/Spouse abuse
	
	-Yelling
		-Preoccupation with illness
		(intolerant of/dwelling on minor ailments)
		
		-Frequent illness
		
		-Physical exhaustion
		
		-Use of self-medication
		
		-Somatic indicators
		  Headache
		  Insomnia
		    initial insomnia
		    recurrent awakening
		    early morning rising
		
		-Change in appetite
		  Weight gain
		  Weight loss
		
		-Indigestion
		
		-Nausea
		
		-Vomiting
		
		-Diarrhea
		
		-Constipation
		
		-Sexual Difficulties
		
		-Sweating

Now we that we know what stress really is and how to recognize our reactions to stress, how do we manage our stress? Let's go on to the next page to discuss *Managing Stress*.

Goal #3: Managing Stress
Some useful things to try when I feel my boat is sinking!

This section covers some useful *"real world"* strategies to help you manage the stresses you feel in your life as a parent. The tools we will discuss include:

> *Avoiding unhealthy ways we cope with stress*

> *What you think really matters: The way our thoughts impact our stress levels*

> *Some "Low Cost" ways to manage your reaction to stress*

>> *Ways to manage your thoughts*

>> *Replacing "untrue" thoughts with "true" ones – ways to keep from making stressful situations even more stressful*

>> *Starting your body's "Relaxation Response"*

>> *Deep breathing exercise*

Let's go to the next page to get started!

☹ *EXAMPLES OF UNHEALTHY COPING METHODS* ☹
☹ ☹ ☹ ☹ ☹ ☹

Even though everyone gets stressed in their own way, there are some common things we can all do to respond to our stress and to manage the difficulties in our lives. Unfortunately, we often try to manage our stress in unhealthy ways, like the ones listed below:

<u>Alcohol</u>: Drinking to change your mood. Using alcohol as your friend.

<u>Denial</u>: Pretending nothing's wrong. Lying. Ignoring your problems.

<u>Drugs</u>: Abusing coffee/aspirin/medications. Smoking pot or cigarettes. Pills. Cocaine.

<u>Eating</u>: Binge eating. Dieting. Using food for comfort.

<u>Fault-Finding</u>: Judging people. Complaining. Criticizing. Blaming others.

<u>Indulging</u>: Staying up late. Sleeping in. Impulse shopping. Wasting time.

<u>Passivity</u>: Procrastinating. Waiting for a lucky break.

<u>Revenge</u>: Getting even. Being sarcastic. Talking mean.

<u>Stubbornness</u>: Being rigid. Demanding your way. Refusing to be wrong.

<u>Tantrums</u>: Yelling. Moping. Pouting. Swearing. Driving recklessly.

<u>Withdrawal</u>: Avoiding the problem. Skipping school/work. Hiding feelings. Over-working

<u>Worrying</u>: Fretting over things. Imagining the worst.

The problem with using *UNHEALTHY COPING METHODS* like these is that they tend to *come at very high cost* to us. We really need to have some tools that are easy to use and that don't cause us more problems than they solve. The next couple of pages should help you develop those tools.

GRANDMA ALWAYS SAID "AN OUNCE OF PREVENTION CAN BE WORTH A POUND OF CURE!"

☆ *Remember the lesson we learned from this story in Chapter 2:*

A famous poem tells a story about a village that sits on the edge of a cliff. Day after day people are injured when they fall off the cliff into the valley below. A village meeting is held to discuss ways to solve the problem of people falling off the cliff and two possible solutions emerge:

> ➢ Build a fence,
>
> ### *or*
>
> ➢ *Keep an ambulance in the valley!*

When dealing with the stress of parenting kids with ADD/ADHD, we tend to *keep an ambulance in the valley.* **In other words, we put lots of effort into dealing with problems** *after* **they start. We want to** *avoid doing this* **if we can!**

So the first step is to Prevent Problems *before* **they begin.** *The 7 Easy Ways To Prevent Stress* **are covered on the next page.**

"AN OUNCE OF PREVENTION CAN BE WORTH A POUND OF CURE" – Part 2!

One of the best ways to keep from becoming stressed out is to keep the levels of stress in your life as low as possible. You should become familiar with *The 7 Easy Ways To Prevent Stress*:

The 7 Easy Ways to Prevent Stress

#1 Use Good Parenting Skills: **Using the skills you learned in *Chapter 2 – The Nuts and Bolts of Behavior Management: Teaching New Behaviors to Kids with ADD/ADHD* – can increase your effectiveness and decrease the times when things go badly. These skills include:**

- Ways to change behaviors through using *Clear Requests*
- Targeting *Behavior Goals* with Point Charts
- The *Nuts and Bolts of Building a Point Chart* to use with your child
- *Linking* rewards and consequences to daily Point Chart goals

If you have not read Chapter 2, we urge you to go back and do so as soon as you finish this chapter!

#2 Take Care of Your Relationships: **One of the best ways to keep the stress levels in your life as low as possible is to work on the relationships in your life. Healthy adult relationships will help keep your overall stress levels down and will help you be a more effective parent! A good book that can teach you how to build and keep good adult relationships is *The Seven Principles for Making Marriage Work* by Dr. John Gottman.**

The 7 Easy Ways to Prevent Stress
(continued)

#3 Good Diet: **A good diet helps your body cope with diseases and stress better and generally will make you feel more energetic and healthy. Taking care of your body is vital to effective parenting – your body needs a good diet! When our bodies are not given a healthy diet we have to work harder to get through our day and we will not be as able to fight off illness. Your children need you to be as physically healthy as possible. It's always a very good idea to run your ideas about dieting and changing your diet by your family doctor – remember, your family doctor is an important resource in coping with stress!**

#4 Water: **Most of us don't drink nearly enough water. Our bodies stop working at their best when the water level gets low – even when it only goes down a little bit. When our bodies don't have enough water, our muscles don't work as well as they usually do. More importantly, when our water levels are low, our brains don't work as well, and our ability to manage our emotions and stress in our lives goes down.** *Drinking at least 8-10 cups of water could help prevent these problems. It's a cheap and easy way to prevent stress!*

#5 Exercise: **One of the best ways to keep your body healthy is to exercise regularly. Your doctor will tell you that 15-20 minutes of low impact exercise a day can greatly increase your overall health, help your immune system fight off sickness and can really improve your mood. We will talk about ways that your body and your mind impact each other on the next couple of pages. Remember to talk with your family doctor before beginning a new exercise plan or when changing the exercise program you currently use. Some good exercises might include:**

* Walking
* Golf
* Basketball
* Aerobics
* Water aerobics
* Yoga
* Running
* Tennis

<u>The 7 Easy Ways to Prevent Stress</u>
(continued)

#6 Be Assertive – Not Aggressive

What does "assertive" mean? You are being "assertive" when you stand up for your personal rights and express your thoughts, feelings and beliefs directly, honestly and spontaneously in ways that don't harm others. Assertive people are clear and direct – but they are not aggressive. When you are assertive, you show respect for yourself and for others. Assertive communication will help the people in your life to take responsibility for their actions and choices. Assertive communication allows you to express your negative feelings in healthy ways and will help you avoid the buildup of resentment. This in turn will help you keep situations from being more stressful than they need to be and will often prevent negative situations altogether. Compare the *aggressive* and *assertive* statements below, and imagine how it would feel to hear each one.

<u>Example of *Aggressive* Statement</u>:
"I *hate* trying to talk to you when you're angry!"

<u>Example of *Assertive* Statement</u>:
"I find it hard to talk with you when you are so upset."

#7 Get Organized: The Joy of Time Management

One of the most common causes of stress is being disorganized. Here are some ways to help prevent stress by getting your life to run more smoothly:

- Make lists
- Put important things at the top of the list
- Learn to say "No"; avoid scheduling too many things
- Schedule breaks – we all need them
- Avoid big decisions when stressed

Let's go on to the next page to learn how the management of our thoughts can help us manage our stress levels.

What You Think Really Matters – The Connections Between Our Minds and Our Bodies!

The *way we think* about things has a lot to do with *how we feel* about them.

The way we think about things really matters because:

Our minds are connected to our bodies.

Alarming thinking often leads to increased stress and even to depression.

Increased stress can cause us to get feel physically bad, and may cause us to get sick more often.

We will explain these ideas over the next couple of pages. We will then discuss ways to use this knowledge to help you manage your stress better, especially when dealing with kids with ADD/ADHD who struggle with *SHOOTING FROM THE HIP, PUTTING ON THE BRAKES,* and *MISSING THE IMPORTANT THINGS.* Let's read on and find out how to bring more peace to our parenting!

Please go on to the next page.

The Connections Between Our Minds and Our Bodies

(continued)

<u>Our minds are connected to our bodies</u>. **This is so true that we'll bet you can think of dozens of examples of ways in which our minds and bodies are connected.**

Our minds can change how our bodies feel: Think about how your body would change if you were in these situations:

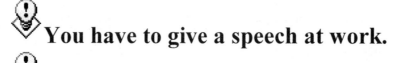

You have to give a speech at work.

You want to ask an attractive person out on a date.

You want to ask your boss for a raise.

You are worrying about how your kid is doing in school.

How would your body react to these situations? Your body would probably do all or some of these things:

- **Your heart rate might speed up.**
- **Your breathing might speed up.**
- **Your neck might hurt.**
- **You may get a headache.**
- **You may get a stomachache.**
- **You might feel hot.**
- **You might feel cold and clammy.**

Our bodies can change our moods: **Think about how your mood would change if you were in these situations:**

 You have the flu.

 You have a toothache.

 You hit your thumb with a hammer.

How would your mood react to these situations? Because of the way your body feels, your mood might change in the following ways:

- **You might become grumpy.**
- **You might feel angry.**
- **You might feel sad.**
- **You might feel frustrated.**

As you can see, your mind can change how your body feels, and your body can change your mood (how your mind feels). Recognizing this can help you manage your stress better.

Alarming thinking often leads to increased stress and even to depression. **When we get really alarmed and begin to think about all the terrible ways that things could go wrong, our stress level almost always goes up and things can become harder than they have to be.**

Some of the ways our thoughts can make things worse include times when:

 We make things bigger than they really are.

 We take things personally.

 We believe that nothing is in our control.

If we allow our thoughts to keep our stress levels rising, then we may eventually begin to believe:

- **Things are bad.**
- **Things have always been bad.**
- **Things are never going to change.**

When these thoughts set in, they are *usually not true* and *not accurate*. Thinking things like that over and over almost always makes things worse.

If the stress and the untrue and inaccurate thoughts continue, depression may eventually set in. Depressed people begin to think:

Bad things are going to happen, and nothing can be done about it – the outcome can't be changed.

Feelings of helplessness and hopelessness eventually creep in and things begin to look dark and bleak.

How does knowing about the relationship between our thoughts and our stress level help us? Let's go on to the next page to learn about some *Low Cost and Effective Ways To Manage Stress.*

$ LOW COST WAYS TO MANAGE STRESS $

Develop strategies that you can use in the moment. Healthy lifestyle changes like a good diet, taking care of your relationships, and exercise are good ways to prevent and manage stress in your life. But what about those times when you can't take the time to run to the gym, take a walk, or talk to a friend? Those are the times you need really good tools that *you can use in the moment* and that *don't take a lot of time.* Let's talk about some ways to do this.

1. **Manage Your Thoughts!** Remember that the way that we make sense of the situations we are in really has a lot to do with how we end up feeling. Think about this story:

   ✓ Three ladies get on a bus in New York City.

   ✓ The bus driver says, "Pay your money, sit down and shut the %*!@# up!"

   ✓ One lady is offended by the bus driver and thinks he is very rude. She decides to write his name down and report him.

   ✓ The second lady is coming from a job interview that did not go well, so she doesn't really hear what the bus driver says.

   ✓ The third lady thinks, "It's GREAT TO BE BACK IN NEW YORK!

The bus driver was the same in each situation. However, the way each lady felt depended on the *meaning* that was given to the bus driver's behavior.

$ LOW COST WAYS TO MANAGE STRESS $
(continued)

2. **Replace Inaccurate or Untrue Thoughts with Accurate and True Ones!** If you hear yourself thinking words like "always," "never," "can't" or "won't," the odds are your thoughts are inaccurate or untrue. Reality check your thoughts! Make sure you are not making things harder than they have to be by over-focusing on the negatives and making things bigger than they really are. A couple of handy ways to pull this off are:

> **Is your glass half empty or half full?** Remember to spend at least as much time thinking about the positive things in your life as you do thinking about the negatives.

> **Use *Thought Stopping*** when you're locked into thinking negative thoughts. If you hear yourself running the same negative thoughts over and over again in your head, simply tell yourself "NO! I'm not going to think that!" If you are alone, say this out loud. If you are in a public setting simply say it in your head (Note: You probably don't want to suddenly shout "No!" in situations where other people are present. They may not understand!) ☺

> **Replace "Un-True" thoughts with accurate "True Thoughts":** When we are alarmed, we begin to think about things as if they are set in stone. We begin to think things like:

>> "I can't handle this anymore!"
>> "He always leaves the toilet seat up!"
>> "She never does what I tell her to do!"

> These statements are absolute and are almost never true. For example, if the man in the second example has *ever* put the toilet seat down, that statement is just not true! If the girl in the third example has *ever* minded when told what to do, then that is also an untrue or inaccurate thought. In other words, these thoughts are probably worse than the situations. We can keep our stress

levels from becoming higher by replacing those "un-true" thoughts with more accurate or true ones like:

"Un-True" Thought: I can't handle this anymore!
True thought: This is really hard for me!

"Un-True" Thought: He always leaves the toilet seat up!
True thought: He sometimes leaves the toilet seat up!

"Un-True" Thought: She never does what I tell her to do!
True thought: She almost never does what I tell her to do!

Do you see the difference? The untrue thoughts make it seem like things are set in stone and there is nothing we can do – the situation is hopeless. The true thoughts are accurate and descriptive – not hopeless! True thoughts empower us to make changes that can improve situations and make things easier and less stressful.

Stay in the moment: We often fail to fully enjoy the good things going on around us when we focus on the bad things that may happen next, or the bad things that have happened before. When we do this, we don't get the "battery charge" out of the good things that we need in order to manage our lives and to be as happy as possible. So we want to stay "in the moment" and enjoy the good things while they are going on. Worrying about bad things doesn't prevent them from happening and but can suck the joy out of the good moments. This idea is captured in an old Native American saying:

"Feast today and remember it tomorrow when you're hungry."

$ LOW COST WAYS TO MANAGE STRESS $
(continued)

3. **Start your body's "Relaxation Response" in stressful situations.** When situations get stressful, our "Fight or Flight" reaction kicks in. The "Fight or Flight" reaction is a natural one that is designed to protect our bodies from physical danger. Our "Fight or Flight" response system is automatic – it kicks in on its own when we are at physical risk. Unfortunately, it also kicks in when we are simply stressed out, so we call it our Stress Response. Our bodies do these things when we are stressed:

 STRESS RESPONSE

Body System	Reaction
Heart	It beats faster and stronger.
Lungs	Breathing becomes faster and shallower.
Muscles	They get tighter (head, shoulders) and may hurt.
Stomach	Digestion is decreased – this leads to stomachaches and indigestion.
Adrenal Gland	Increased adrenaline revs up our minds and our bodies.
Immune System	It gets worn down and we get sick!

While this process is automatic, we can turn on our Relaxation Response in a couple of different ways. Please go to the next page to learn how to turn off your body's Stress Response and turn on its Relaxation Response!

$ LOW COST WAYS TO MANAGE STRESS $
(continued)

 THE RELAXATION RESPONSE: So far, the tools we have discussed have been focused on our thoughts and the way we can make ourselves feel better emotionally and physically by managing our thinking. Now we are going to give you a tool that will help your body turn on its natural **Relaxation Response**. This tool could also help with your emotional and physical well-being!

 Remember that our Stress Response is automatic: It kicks in when we are physically threatened and can be really helpful in some situations, such as when a car pulls out in front of you in traffic. Unfortunately, the Stress Response also kicks in when we are under emotional threat – like when the boss yells at us or when our children don't mind. When the "Fight or Flight" part of our Stress Response kicks in, it simply makes stressful situations more stressful. Luckily our bodies also have a natural **Relaxation Response** that we can help get going in stressful situations by simply controlling our breathing. On the next page we describe what happens when the natural **Relaxation Response** kicks in!

Please go on to the next page.

$ LOW COST WAYS TO MANAGE STRESS $

(continued)

As you can see by looking at the table below, when the *Relaxation Response* kicks in, the revving up done by the body during the *Stress Response* settles down. This allows the body to move into a more peaceful and calm mode.

THE RELAXATION RESPONSE

Body System	Reaction
Heart	It slows down and becomes more regular.
Lungs	Breathing becomes slower and deeper.
Muscles	They loosen and a sense of physical relief can set in.
Stomach	Digestion increases and stomachaches or uncomfortable feelings decrease.
Adrenal Gland	The body releases chemicals that cancel out the adrenaline – increasing a calming effect to the body and the mind.
Immune System	It has a chance to recharge and get stronger, thus helping us to fight off bugs and avoid getting sick.

The Relaxation Response can be turned on by doing the brief breathing exercise on the next page. It's simple, fast and easy!

DEEP BREATHING EXERCISE

Take a few minutes and try this simple exercise. It will turn off the *Stress Response* and turn on your Relaxation Response. It is a nice way to catch a break during the day or after some stressful parenting time!

DEEP BREATHING EXERCISE

1. **Sit in a comfortable position:** Don't cross your legs or arms – this cuts off blood flow and can make your Stress Response start up. It's best to sit with your arms on your thighs or on the arms of the chair and with both feet flat on the floor.

2. **Take 3 deep cleansing breaths:** This means you want to breathe in for 2-4 seconds, hold your breath for 2-3 seconds, and then breathe out for 4-6 seconds while trying to force all the air out of your body. It's best if you breathe in through your nose and out through your mouth.

3. **Try to breathe so that only your stomach rises and falls:** This is a natural way to breathe – slow and deep. However, most of us breathe rapidly and take shallow breaths from our chest. Remember that rapid and shallow breathing is part of the Stress Response; long slow breaths are part of the Relaxation Response. Athletes and singers often try to breathe this way. (It's called breathing from the diaphragm.)

   As you inhale, concentrate on your chest remaining relatively still while your stomach rises. It may be helpful to imagine that your pants are too big and you need to push your stomach out to hold them up.

4. **Take 5 minutes for slow relaxing breaths, continuing to breathe so that only your stomach moves:** Try to breathe deeply and slowly while imagining that your body is heavy and sinking deeper and deeper into the chair. Close your eyes and think about the word CALM while concentrating on relaxing your body. The word CALM will help you remember to relax the different parts of your body. (Turn the page to learn how ☺.)

DEEP BREATHING EXERCISE
(continued)

5. **The CALM reminder:** While taking slow and deep breaths, the word **CALM** will help remind you to relax some of the major parts of your body. As you can see below, each letter in the word stands for a different body part.

   Chest: Breathing slower and deeper
   Arms: Shoulders sag
   Legs: Loose and flexible
   Mouth: Jaw drops open slightly

   When you close your eyes and think or say the word **CALM**, imagine all the stress or tension leaving your body as you exhale. Each time you exhale you may feel your body becoming a bit more relaxed. Sometimes this exercise can be even better if you spend time thinking about peaceful things. A really good thing to do is to picture the peaceful place in your mind as completely as possible.

---

6. **Try to practice this breathing exercise at least once or twice a day:** Remember that *taking care of you* is very important. This is a quick and easy way to give your body and your mind a break. Don't convince yourself that you are too busy to practice some stress management – your kids need you healthy and rested!

Please go to the next page to read a summary of this chapter and a preview of Chapter 6.

Chapter Summary/Preview of Chapter 6

Congratulations **on finishing this very important chapter on *What to Do When the Kids Are Driving You Nuts: Stress Management for Parents.* You should now have a pretty good handle on:**

- *Understanding* stress

- *Recognizing* stress

- *Managing* Stress

    - Avoiding Unhealthy Coping Methods

    - Preventing Stress – "An Ounce of Prevention"

    - The 7 Easy Ways to Prevent Stress

    - What You Think Really Matters – The Connection Between Our Minds and Bodies

    - Low Cost Ways to Manage Stress

We hope you have found the tools in this chapter helpful. We invite you to continue on to *Chapter #6: Involvement and Communication: Two Antidotes for Low Self-Esteem.*

Chapter 6 Will Focus on the Following Tools:

- *Unhealthy Family Habits That Can Hurt Self-Esteem*

- *The 6 Steps to Effective Encouragement — the Key to Good Self-Esteem*

- *Child-Directed Play: A Good Self-Esteem Builder*

- *Problem Solving Through Negotiation*

- *Getting to Know Your Child's School Life*

CHAPTER 6:
Involvement and Communication: Two Antidotes for Low Self-Esteem

Involvement and Communication: Two Antidotes for Low Self-Esteem

Introduction

We have covered a lot of information in this manual. Topics covered so far have included understanding what ADD/ADHD is and what it isn't; useful teaching tools; healthy discipline techniques; teaching kids with ADD/ADHD how to get and stay organized, and stress management tools for parents. This final chapter stresses the ways that you can have a positive impact on your child with ADD/ADHD by breaking bad family habits, focusing on good communication within your family and by being actively involved in all parts of your child's life. Doing everything possible to improve self-esteem, self-confidence and problem solving abilities is especially important for kids with ADD/ADHD, who typically struggle with *SHOOTING FROM THE HIP, PUTTING ON THE BRAKES* and *MISSING THE IMPORTANT THINGS*. We hope you will find the tools in this final chapter to be useful and helpful.

Let's go to the next page to view our Road Map to Chapter 6.

ROAD MAP TO CHAPTER 6

<u>THINGS WE ARE GOING TO COVER IN THIS CHAPTER</u>

You are about to begin a critical chapter on the ways that good communication and family involvement in your child's life can lead to good self-esteem, self-confidence, and problem solving. The areas we will cover are listed below.

- *Unhealthy Family Habits That Can Hurt Self-Esteem*
- *Breaking Unhealthy Family Habits to Help Improve Good Self-Esteem in Kids*
- *The 6 Steps to Effective Encouragement – the Key To Good Self-Esteem*
- *Child-Directed Play: A Good Self-Esteem Builder*
- *Problem Solving Through Negotiation*
- *Getting to Know Your Child's School Life*
- *Promoting School Success*
- *Working Together as a Team*

☺ Let's get started! ☺

124

Unhealthy Habits Start When Family Members Treat One Another in Unpleasant Ways

Unhealthy or Bad Habits: **Families have habits just like individual people have habits. This is true of families in general and especially in families who are helping children who struggle with** *SHOOTING FROM THE HIP, PUTTING ON THE BRAKES* **and** *MISSING THE IMPORTANT THINGS.* **Some habits like the ones below are good and healthy ones:**

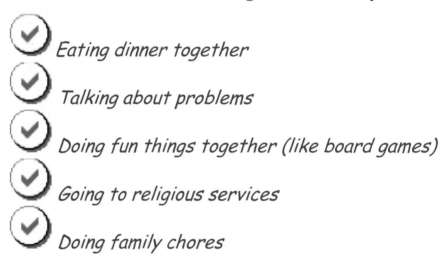

Some families develop habits that are not so healthy and are often painful to all family members. Some examples of unhealthy and painful habits are:

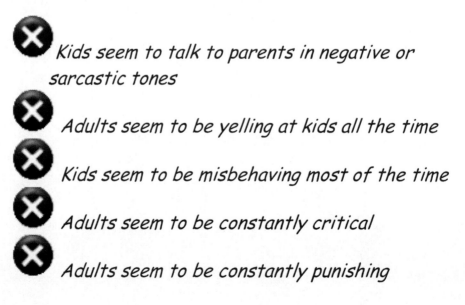

Negative Habits
(Continued)

When unhealthy, bad and painful family habits set in, things can get to a point where most family members cause each other *lots of emotional pain.* When this happens, many family members may start *avoiding the pain of being with one another.* When these habits develop, a couple of things may begin to happen in the family:

- *Family members begin to use pain to get the things they need from other family members*

- *Family members begin to give in to one another to avoid pain*

- *Family members begin to dislike each other*

- *Family members may become hopeless and may begin to feel helpless to change things*

- *The self-esteem of the kids in the family may be damaged*

When unhealthy or bad habits develop, they can be especially damaging for families of children who struggle with *SHOOTING FROM THE HIP, PUTTING ON THE BRAKES* and *MISSING THE IMPORTANT THINGS.*

What can we do about this? Let's go to the next page to discuss some ways to drop these bad or unhealthy family habits.

126

Breaking Bad Family Habits Can Help Kids' Self-Esteem, Self-Confidence And Problem Solving

---

The development of good self-esteem, high self-confidence and good problem solving skills in kids with ADD/ADHD is essential. These skills are important because *self-confident children tend to make better decisions* **when we (parents) are not around.**

Self-confident children with good self-esteem and good problem solving skills will be more successful in many ways, including:

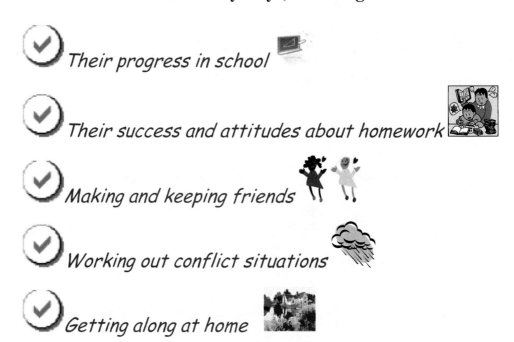

✅ *Their progress in school*

✅ *Their success and attitudes about homework*

✅ *Making and keeping friends*

✅ *Working out conflict situations*

✅ *Getting along at home*

 Let's go on to the next page to learn some specific ways to break the Bad Habit Cycle.

Some Specific Ways to Break the Bad Habit Cycle

There are a number of ways to break the *Bad Habit Cycle* in your family. As we mentioned on the last page, this is especially important for families who are trying to help their children with ADD/ADHD. Many of the tools we learned in earlier chapters will go a long way toward dropping the bad habits that can develop in our families. Let's review those here.

#1 *Targeting Behavior Goals by Using Tracking Forms and Point Charts:* **These help us to**

☆ *Notice* **the things our kids do.**

☆ *Teach* **our kids by giving tools to provide feedback.**

☆ *Rewards*
☆ *Discipline/Negative Consequences*

☆ *Slow The World Down* **so learning can happen.**

#2 *Rewarding:* **Creating a high ratio of positive to negative interactions helps kids to feel empowered to try, and to feel good about their efforts.**

#3 *Making effective requests:* **This eliminates misunderstanding and should decrease the overall stress level in your family, increase the number of times things go well in your family, and really help your child's self-esteem.**

#4 *Personal Stress Management:* **The tools you learned in Chapter 5 will help to minimize the negative emotions in the family and will keep parents in a "teaching mode" rather than an emotional one.**

128

 Some Other Ways to Break the Bad Habit Cycle

On the next several pages we will cover some additional ways to break the Bad Habit Cycles that may have developed in your family. We will cover the following tools:

 Effective encouragement – a "how to" section. This will give you a "nuts and bolts" way to keep up the positives in your kid's life.

 Enhancement of child self-esteem through Child-Directed Play. This section teaches how to sometimes let your child be in charge when you play together. This will help build confidence and self esteem.

 Problem solving through negotiation. This section will help you teach your kids the negotiation skills they will need to be successful at school, home and later in adulthood.

 Knowing your child's school life. Your kids spend a huge amount of time at school. This section will remind you to get to know that part of their world and the challenges they face there.

 Family, school, psychologist and physician working as a team. This section will encourage you to take a "team approach" to help your kids with ADD/ADHD as they struggle with *SHOOTING FROM THE HIP, PUTTING ON THE BRAKES* and *MISSING THE IMPORTANT THINGS.*

Effective Encouragement –the Key to Success

The *Keys to Effective Encouragement* are very similar to the *Clear Requests* tools you learned in Chapter 2. The steps are listed in the table below and then explained in more detail on later pages. Think about each step as you encourage and praise your kids.

The 6 Steps to Effective Encouragement

1. **Make eye contact**

2. **Be specific**

3. **Praise immediately and often**

4. **Smile, hug and be enthusiastic**

5. **Be consistent**

6. **No negative "trailers" (e.g., "Good job making your bed...now why can't you do that all the time?")**

Before going on, think about the following examples of good and healthy statements and remember that frequent encouragement can help break the Bad Habit cycles in your family.

Examples of Encouraging Statements:

1. **"Thanks for doing that so quickly."**

2. **"You're doing a nice job of coloring!"**

3. **"Thank you for sharing."**

4. **"Mommy's proud of you for...."**

The 6 Steps to Effective Encouragement - Explained

1. *Make eye contact:* We spend a lot of time talking to the tops, sides and backs of kids' heads. If we don't have their eyes, we probably don't have their attention. If we don't have their attention, then they may be *Missing Important Things* – like the encouragement you are giving them!

2. *Be specific:* Make sure your kids realize that you know *they have good ideas*, that you believe *they are important*, and that you believe *they can accomplish the things they set out to do.*

3. *Praise immediately and often:* Don't put it off! Praise is most effective if it happens right after kids put in their efforts. Don't be stingy; Dr. Al calls it "Noticing their success with your mouth."

4. *Smile, hug and be enthusiastic:* Enjoy your kids! Enjoy being with them…enjoy teaching them…enjoy watching them grow and change.

5. *Be consistent:* This makes life predictable and helps kids feel confident and safe. Consistent praise teaches our kids what to do – and there is no more important lesson in life!

6. *No negative "trailers":* This is a negative trailer: "Good job making your bed…now why can't you do that all the time? We wouldn't have these problems if you would just do this all the time, %!#&@$!" Would you feel praised if this was said to you, or would you feel punished? If you are adding negative trailers, your stress level is probably too high. Please see Chapter 5 for some helpful hints on managing stress.

Let's go on to learn about Child-Directed Play

ENHANCEMENT OF CHILD SELF-ESTEEM: CHILD-DIRECTED PLAY

One of the ways we can help our kids be more self-confident is to give them opportunities to be in charge when we are playing with them. What we mean by "be in charge" is simply allowing the child to direct the activities you are doing for a brief period – within reason. This will give your kids the opportunity to feel what it's like to be the boss, in a safe and educational way.

Think about those times when you are trying to "bring along" new people at work. You often will let them be in charge, but will do so in ways that protect them from the dangers of making a big mistake. Very Special Time is a tool that can help you do this for your kids.

VERY SPECIAL TIME: VST

What exactly is VST? VST is simply a 10-15 minute period of time spent with your child each day during which she or he is the BOSS!

During VST, the following things need to happen:

1. Your child receives your complete and undivided attention.

2. She/he is the boss. You do whatever your child wants and are involved to the extent that she or he wants you to be.

During VST the child has only to follow three simple rules:

1. The child cannot choose to do anything that is harmful to self or others (no hitting or jumping off the roof, for example).

2. The child cannot choose to do anything that is destructive to property.

3. VST must take place in the home or in the yard. Going places is special to the child, but it creates a "load" situation where the parent needs to be in charge.
   The goal is to allow the child to be in charge!

⭐ Making VST Go Smoothly ⭐

1. *Explain Very Special Time.* **Walk through it with your children. The exact instructions for VST are listed below:**

   Step #1: **Say "Today we will be doing Very Special Time."**

   Step #2: **Say "During Very Special Time we will do whatever activity you choose for the next 15 minutes."**

   Step #3: **Say "There are only a couple of rules we have to follow."**

   Step #4: **Say "You cannot choose to do anything that is harmful to you or to others (things like hitting or jumping off the roof)."**

   Step #5: **Say "You may not choose to do anything that is destructive to property."**

   Step #6: **Say "This is an activity that we can only do at home."**

   Step #7: **Say "Do you have any questions?"**

   Step #8: **Say "Let's get started!"**

2. *Misbehavior:* **The child is misbehaving only if he or she violates one of the three rules discussed above. If this happens:**

   *Warn the child that if the behavior continues, VST will end. (Note: *Automatically* end VST if the behavior is harmful or dangerous).

   *Walk out if behavior continues...this terminates VST.

   *Don't discuss it with the child...let the consequence work.

☆ Making VST Go Smoothly ☆
(continued)

3. *Involve all adults in the home.* This can be fun for everyone and can be good for your child's relationships with all adults in your home.

4. *REMEMBER, IT'S SUPPOSED TO BE POSITIVE:* If it becomes or seems to be negative, do some reality checking. Talk to your partner or other parents and discuss what you are doing.

Before you begin VST with your child, make sure to review the list of DOs and DON'Ts we have provided below. Remember that you are placing your child in charge during VST, so don't place demands on her or him. Even simple things like asking questions places a demand on the child; if you ask a question, the child is obligated to answer it. So just do the things in the "DOs" list below and you will be fine!

DOs and DON'Ts of Very Special Time

DO	*DON'T*
Praise	Criticize
Describe	Command
Reflect	Question
Imitate	Control

Final Word on VST: **It's best to have a couple of regularly scheduled VST appointments with your kid throughout the week. VST should increase the number of times you have fun with your kid and should certainly help with the development of self-confidence and self-esteem.**

PROBLEM SOLVING THROUGH NEGOTIATION

All children need to have good negotiation and problem solving skills. These skills are often difficult to develop. This can be especially true for kids who struggle with ADD/ADHD and who may have difficulties with *SHOOTING FROM THE HIP, PUTTING ON THE BRAKES* and *MISSING THE IMPORTANT THINGS.* This brief section will review some basic problem solving and negotiation tools that you can use with your kids. These steps are very similar to those being taught in businesses around the world every day!

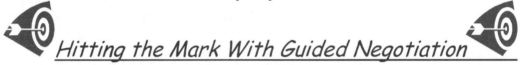

Hitting the Mark With Guided Negotiation

Instructions: **Please follow these simple steps when negotiating or problem solving with your kids.**

1. *Clearly state the problem:* **Clearly describe the issue you are negotiating. Make sure that you follow the steps below:**

   → **Be short**

   → **Be specific**

   → **Avoid criticism**

2. *Brainstorm solutions:* **Try to draw out ideas from your kids. This communicates that you value them and you think they have good ideas. This can be a delightful activity if you manage your stress well and if you try to have fun with it. Remember to do the following things when brainstorming:**

   → **Treat all ideas as good ideas**

   → **Try to use humor and have fun**

   → **Write the ideas down**

3. *Evaluate solutions:* **This is the time to go through all the ideas and to keep the realistic ones and cross off the ones that just won't work. Remember to stay positive and to keep your sense of humor as you do this.**

> → **Cross out or combine ideas**

> → **Discuss advantages and disadvantages before deciding to keep or cross off any idea**

4. *PICK A SOLUTION:* **This is where you decide, as a family, on one of the solutions that has not been crossed off the list. If the family cannot decide, it is OK for the parents to simply select the one they feel is best. However, reaching a family agreement is usually much better.**

5. *Write an agreement:* **Once you have picked a solution, write down the steps involved in accomplishing the task. Try to be as specific as possible – include steps, completion times, etc. It is also very important to include the consequences of accomplishing the task: the rewards. You should also include the consequences of failing to complete the task: discipline or punishment. When writing down your agreement you want it to be:**

> → **So clear that a visitor to your house would understand it.**

> → **Posted so you and your kids can see it easily.**

6. *Pick a date to review the solution:* **Pick a day that you and your child can sit down to review the solution and assess how well it's working. If everything is working well, keep the solution. If it's not working well, you may need to modify the solution or repeat the process and try a different solution.**

On the next page we discuss ways to get to know your child's school life

What I Know About My Kid's School Life

Knowing what goes on in the lives of your children when you are away from them will give you insight into the challenges they face each and every day. Understanding their school world will allow you to see the ways that you can help your children be as successful as possible. Becoming involved in your children's school lives will show them you care, and that you are a helpful resource for them when they struggle. Now would be a good time to ask yourself how much you know about your children's school lives.

Do you know the answers to the following questions?

My Child's School

Your child spends a significant amount of time each day at school – almost as much as many adults spend at work. The only way to truly understand the struggles and successes in your child's life is to get to know the school. So, ask yourself:

Do I know....

The teacher's name?

The number of children in the class?

The schedule of daily activities?

Where my child sits in the classroom?

What time my child eats lunch?

What time my child has recess?

Who my child's friends are?

What I Know About My Kid's School Life
(continued)

My Child

Do you know the things your children like and dislike at school? Do you know what subjects they enjoy, and which ones are difficult or boring for them? Do you know how your children learn and how they interact with the educational system at their school? Do you know how they solve problems at school when they arise? Understanding these things about your children can help you appreciate their world more completely. Ask yourself the following:

Do I know...

My child's favorite subject?

My child's least favorite subject?

If my child volunteers to answer questions in class?

What my child does when he/she doesn't understand something?

What my child does if a classmate is being annoying?

If my child is having problems with any classmates?

Homework

Understanding how your children manage their homework will help you to understand how they handle school. Ask yourself:

Do I know...

What homework my child has each night?

If my child has completed the assigned homework each night?

If my child turns in the homework when he/she gets to school?

What the teacher does if my child doesn't turn in homework?

PROMOTING SCHOOL SUCCESS

Here are four ways to improve your child's success at school. It's good to be involved before problems creep up. Teachers appreciate parents who are involved.

1. COMMUNICATE WITH THE TEACHER

This person spends a large number of hours with your child five days a week and in many different situations. *Calling your child's teacher* is a great way to have direct contact. You might also *write a note* to the teacher sharing any concerns you may have. You can mail it directly, e-mail it or send it to school with your child. One of our favorites is the *daily school report card* – a great way to get information regularly! (See Chapter 2 for examples.)

2. OBSERVE DIRECTLY

Visiting your child's classroom provides a direct source of invaluable information. *Most teachers enjoy having parents visit* if arrangements have been made beforehand. When you're right there in class, you'll get a better picture of what your child is asked to do and how she or he works with others.

3. ASK YOUR CHILD

Ask your child specific questions about what happened in school. *This is a time to devote your full attention to what your child is saying.* Make sure you have 5 minutes when you are not reading the paper, watching TV, cooking or repairing something. *You need to be able to listen.* If you don't quite understand what you child is saying, ask another question. Avoid interrupting or over-interpreting what your child is saying.

4. CREATE A DAILY ROUTINE

Setting aside a certain time and place each day is a good way for children to begin forming good study habits. On the next page you will find some hints for creating a daily routine in your own home.

CREATING A DAILY ROUTINE

This page contains a brief checklist that will help you form a daily routine with your child. Remember that children who struggle with *SHOOTING FROM THE HIP, PUTTING ON THE BRAKES* and *MISSING THE IMPORTANT THINGS* need structure and consistency in order to be as successful as possible.

1. PROVIDE A GOOD SETTING FOR STUDYING

   Where: _____

2. MAKE A REGULAR STUDY TIME A PRIORITY

   When: _____

3. BE PRESENT DURING STUDY TIME

   Who: _____

4. ENCOURAGE READ AND STUDY TIME FIVE DAYS A WEEK

   How: _____

WORKING TOGETHER AS A TEAM

Finally, children with ADD/ADHD need the adults in their lives to work together. This is best done when we draw the child, the family, the school, psychologists, social workers and physicians together to work as a team. This page contains some helpful hints about how to make that happen.

1. FOSTER OPEN COMMUNICATION

2. DON'T ALLOW TURF ISSUES TO GET IN THE WAY

3. UNDERSTAND THE FRUSTRATION OF OTHER PEOPLE

4. TRUST YOUR EXPERTS:

   -PARENTS ARE EXPERTS ON THEIR CHILD

   -TEACHERS ARE DEVELOPMENTAL EXPERTS

   -PHYSICIANS ARE EXPERTS ON MEDICATIONS

   -PSYCHOLOGISTS/THERAPISTS ARE BEHAVIORAL EXPERTS

5. COORDINATE YOUR EFFORTS...IF WE FAIL AT THE TASKS IN 1-4 ABOVE, WHO PAYS?

Congratulations on finishing the last chapter of our text. This chapter covered a number of very important ways to have positive impact on your kid's self-esteem, including:

- *Unhealthy Family Habits That Can Hurt Self-Esteem*

- *Breaking Unhealthy Family Habits to Help Improve Good Self-Esteem in Kids*

- *The 6 Steps to Effective Encouragement – the Key to Good Self-Esteem*

- *Child-Directed Play: A Good Self-Esteem Builder*

- *Problem Solving Through Negotiation*

- *Getting to Know Your Child's School Life*

- *Promoting School Success*

- *Working Together as a Team*

We truly hope you have found this chapter, as well as the entire manual, to be useful to you as you strive to help your kids with ADD/ADHD. We know that kids who struggle with *SHOOTING FROM THE HIP, PUTTING ON THE BRAKES* and *MISSING THE IMPORTANT THINGS* have special needs, and we truly admire you for doing all that you can to learn the best ways to help your child to be successful.

FINAL NOTES

Thanks so much for taking the time to read this text. Dr. Al Winebarger and the entire staff at Parmelee and Winebarger Psychological Consulting have put a tremendous amount of effort into creating a manual that is useful to real parents of real kids with ADD/ADHD living in the real world.

The Appendix contains a list of sources used in the writing of this manual and a list of books where you can learn more information in greater detail. If you have any suggestions for ways to improve this volume or have any specific questions about the ideas in it, please feel free to contact Dr. Al via e-mail at DocAl@charter.net or by telephone at (616) 842-4772. Also feel free to write to Dr. Al or any of the staff at Parmelee and Winebarger Psychological Consulting at:

Parmelee and Winebarger Psychological Consulting
321 Fulton Street
Grand Haven, MI 49417

Appendix

This Appendix contains copies of the forms necessary to build the behavior management/Point Chart system described in Chapter 2 *(The Nuts and Bolts of Behavior Management: Teaching New Behaviors to Kids with ADD/ADHD)*. **The forms presented here fall into two categories:**

1. POINT CHART WORKSHEETS, SAMPLE POINT CHARTS AND BLANK POINT CHARTS (see pages 32 – 40 in Chapter 2)

and

2. SAMPLE SCHOL CARDS AND BLANK SCHOOL CARDS (see pages 42 – 43 in Chapter 2)

POINT CHART WORKSHEETS, SAMPLE POINT CHARTS AND BLANK POINT CHARTS

This section contains:

1. *Point Chart Worksheet:* This form helps you break down behavior goals down into the steps that can be added to the Point Chart. Two blank copies of this form are included.

2. *Sample Point Charts:* We have given you two completed sample Point Charts similar to those used daily in our office. These will give you ideas for building a personalized Point Chart to use with your child.

3. *Blank Point Charts:* We have provided two copies of a blank Point Chart that you may fill in by hand, after you have identified the Behavior Goals and broken them down into their steps. Remember to make the point totals add up to 100 possible points per day. Good luck!

Remember: If you have any difficulty using the forms in this section, or applying the lessons in Chapter 2, make sure you contact a local psychologist or behavior specialist for assistance.

★ *POINT CHART WORKSHEET* ★

Pick something that you would like to see improved and write it in the space below. We'll call this our *Behavior Goal*. Then break the goal down into very clear parts. Make those parts so clear that strangers would understand them if they had to come and live in your home! Then transfer the *Behavior Goal* and its parts to your Point Chart. (Look in the Appendix to find a blank Point Chart you can use for this purpose). Finally, think about the ways in which you plan to reward your children when they reach the *Behavior Goal*. Then repeat this process for each new goal until you have completed your Point Chart (Look at the Point Charts in this section for ideas if you are stuck).

A. What I'd Like to See Improved – the *Behavior Goal* :

B: List the parts of our *Behavior Goal*. (BE SPECIFIC!):

      1. _____

      2. _____

      3. _____

      4. _____

      5. _____

C. Transfer the *Behavior Goal and the steps* to the Point Chart.

This form should help you get the new behaviors broken down into steps to put on your Point Chart. Remember, there are more of these forms and a blank Point Chart in the Appendix – copy them and use them ☺☺!

★ *POINT CHART WORKSHEET* ★

Pick something that you would like to see improved and then write it in the space below. We'll call this our *Behavior Goal.* **Then break the goal down into very clear parts. Make those parts so clear that strangers would understand them if they had to come and live in your home! Then transfer the** *Behavior Goal* **and its parts to your Point Chart. (Look in the Appendix to find a blank Point Chart you can use for this purpose.) Finally, think about the ways in which you plan to reward your children when they reach the** *Behavior Goal.* **Then repeat this process for each new goal until you have completed your Point Chart (Look at the Point Charts in this section for ideas if you are stuck).**

A. What I'd Like to See Improved – the *Behavior Goal* **:**

B: List the parts of our *Behavior Goal.* **(BE SPECIFIC!):**

1. _____

2. _____

3. _____

4. _____

5. _____

C. Transfer the *Behavior Goal and the steps* **to the Point Chart.**

This form should help you get the new behaviors broken down into steps to put on your point chart. Remember, there are more of these forms and a blank Point Chart in the Appendix – copy them and use them ☺☺!

A SAMPLE POINT CHART

Date:

	Sun	Mon	Tues	Wed	Thurs	Fri	Sat
Getting Ready for School (10 total) -Teeth (2) -Dressed (2) -Covers pulled up on bed (2) -Meds (4)							
Homework/Reading (20 total) (Right after dinner – before playing)							
School Agenda book/School Card (20 total) (Bringing it home)							
Picking Up Room (20 total) -Clothes in basket (4) -Dishes/Food cleaned up (4) -Dresser drawers closed/top tidy (4) -Clothes folded (4) -Clear floor (4) (Before bed)							
Getting Ready for Bed (20 total) -Brushing teeth (5) -In bed by 9 (5) -Lights out by 10 (5) -Family room tidy (put away toys and/or books) (5)							
Pleasant and Polite Attitude (10) total							
Total	/100	/100	/100	/100	/100	/100	/100

SAMPLE POINT CHART

Date:

	Sun	Mon	Tues	Wed	Thurs	Fri	Sat
Pleasant and Polite Attitude (10 total)							
Getting Ready for School -Getting up (2) -Teeth (2) -Dressed in clean clothes (2) -Food (2) -Meds (2) (10 total)							
Read and study when home (5-5:30 p.m.) (20)							
Planner (20) (Bringing it home/signed)							
Evening Chores -Empty trash (daily) -End of drive on Trash Day (by 4:15 p.m.) (10)							
Getting Ready for Bed (20) -Shower/Brushing teeth (5) -Bed on time (5) -PJs (5) -Clothes in hamper (5)							
Total	/100	/100	/100	/100	/100	/100	/100

149

POINT CHART for: _____

Date:

(Fill in goals and points)	Sun	Mon	Tues	Wed	Thurs	Fri	Sat
Total	/100	/100	/100	/100	/100	/100	/100

Date: _____

POINT CHART for: _____

(Fill in goals and points)	Sun	Mon	Tues	Wed	Thurs	Fri	Sat
Total	/100	/100	/100	/100	/100	/100	/100

☆ SCHOOL CARDS ☆

This section has sample and blank School Cards that can be used daily with your child. These school cards fit nicely with the Point Charts listed on earlier pages. This section has five examples of School Cards; each example is followed by blank School Cards you may use to create customized School Cards for your child by simply filling them out. Computer generated file copies of the School Cards and Point Charts may be ordered from our Web site at:

http://www.ARW-Learning.com

SCHOOL CARD FOR ELEMENTARY AGE KIDS

Date: _____

Goals	Before 10 a.m.	After 10 a.m.
On Task	☺ ☺	☺ ☺
Staying in Seat When I'm Supposed to	☺ ☺	☺ ☺
Getting Along With Others	☺ ☺	☺ ☺
Following Directions	☺ ☺	☺ ☺

Note to teacher: Two ☺s = "Great job"; One ☺ = "Good, but could improve"; Zero ☺ = "Needs work."

 SCHOOL CARD FOR ELEMENTARY AGE KIDS

Date: _____

Goals	Before Lunch	After Lunch
On Task	☺ ☺	☺ ☺
Staying in Seat When I'm Supposed to	☺ ☺	☺ ☺
Getting Along With Others	☺ ☺	☺ ☺
Following Directions	☺ ☺	☺ ☺

Note to teacher: Two ☺s = "Great job"; One ☺ = "Good, but could improve"; Zero ☺ = "Needs work."

SCHOOL CARD FOR _____

Date: _____

Goals (fill in)	Before 10 a.m.		After 10 a.m.	
	☺	☺	☺	☺
	☺	☺	☺	☺
	☺	☺	☺	☺
	☺	☺	☺	☺

Note to teacher: Two ☺s = "Great job"; One ☺ = "Good, but could improve"; Zero ☺ = "Needs work."

SCHOOL CARD FOR _____

Date: _____

Goals (fill in)	Before Lunch		After Lunch	
	☺	☺	☺	☺
	☺	☺	☺	☺
	☺	☺	☺	☺
	☺	☺	☺	☺

Note to teacher: Two ☺s = "Great job"; One ☺ = "Good, but could improve"; Zero ☺ = "Needs work."

Sample School Card (includes daycare)

Date:

	Morning	Afternoon	Daycare
Minding	☆ ☆	☆ ☆	☆ ☆
Paying Attention	☆ ☆	☆ ☆	☆ ☆
Being Nice to Animals	☆ ☆	☆ ☆	☆ ☆
Homework, Reading, Writing	☆ ☆	☆ ☆	☆ ☆

 # Sample School Card (includes daycare)

Date:

	Morning	Afternoon	Daycare
Minding	☆ ☆	☆ ☆	☆ ☆
Paying Attention	☆ ☆	☆ ☆	☆ ☆
Being Nice to Animals	☆ ☆	☆ ☆	☆ ☆
Homework, Reading, Writing	☆ ☆	☆ ☆	☆ ☆

Sample School Card (includes daycare)

Date:

Goal (fill in)	Morning	Afternoon	Daycare
	☆ ☆	☆ ☆	☆ ☆
	☆ ☆	☆ ☆	☆ ☆
	☆ ☆	☆ ☆	☆ ☆
	☆ ☆	☆ ☆	☆ ☆

 # Sample School Card (includes daycare)

Date:

Goal (fill in)	Morning	Afternoon	Daycare
	☆ ☆	☆ ☆	☆ ☆
	☆ ☆	☆ ☆	☆ ☆
	☆ ☆	☆ ☆	☆ ☆
	☆ ☆	☆ ☆	☆ ☆

SCHOOL CARD – FOR USE WITH OLDER KIDS

NAME: DATE:

Class/Hour	On Time	Homework Overdue?	Homework Assigned	On Task?	Teacher Initials and Comments
Geometry	YES / NO	YES / NO	YES / NO	YES / NO	
History	YES / NO	YES / NO	YES / NO	YES / NO	
English	YES / NO	YES / NO	YES / NO	YES / NO	
Biology	YES / NO	YES / NO	YES / NO	YES / NO	
German	YES / NO	YES / NO	YES / NO	YES / NO	
Choir	YES / NO	YES / NO	YES / NO	YES / NO	

Note to teacher: Please circle Yes or No in each box, list comments and sign.
Thanks!

SCHOOL CARD – FOR USE WITH OLDER KIDS

NAME: DATE:

Class/Hour	On Time	Homework Overdue?	Homework Assigned	On Task?	Teacher Initials and Comments
Geometry	YES / NO	YES / NO	YES / NO	YES / NO	
History	YES / NO	YES / NO	YES / NO	YES / NO	
English	YES / NO	YES / NO	YES / NO	YES / NO	
Biology	YES / NO	YES / NO	YES / NO	YES / NO	
German	YES / NO	YES / NO	YES / NO	YES / NO	
Choir	YES / NO	YES / NO	YES / NO	YES / NO	

Note to teacher: Please circle Yes or No in each box, list comments and sign.
Thanks!

SCHOOL CARD – FOR: _____ (name)

NAME: DATE:

Class/Hour	On Time	Homework Overdue?	Homework Assigned	On Task?	Teacher Initials and Comments
	YES / NO	YES / NO	YES / NO	YES / NO	
	YES / NO	YES / NO	YES / NO	YES / NO	
	YES / NO	YES / NO	YES / NO	YES / NO	
	YES / NO	YES / NO	YES / NO	YES / NO	
	YES / NO	YES / NO	YES / NO	YES / NO	
	YES / NO	YES / NO	YES / NO	YES / NO	

Note to teacher: Please circle Yes or No in each box, list comments and sign. Thanks!

SCHOOL CARD – FOR: _____ (name)

NAME: DATE:

Class/Hour	On Time	Homework Overdue?	Homework Assigned	On Task?	Teacher Initials and Comments
	YES / NO	YES / NO	YES / NO	YES / NO	
	YES / NO	YES / NO	YES / NO	YES / NO	
	YES / NO	YES / NO	YES / NO	YES / NO	
	YES / NO	YES / NO	YES / NO	YES / NO	
	YES / NO	YES / NO	YES / NO	YES / NO	
	YES / NO	YES / NO	YES / NO	YES / NO	

Note to teacher: Please circle Yes or No in each box, list comments and sign. Thanks!

158

NAME: DATE:

Class/Hour	Polite and Calm	Homework: Overdue?	Works Well with Others	On Task?	Teacher Initials and Comments
Block #1 (Social Studies)	1---2---3	YES / NO	1---2---3	1---2---3	
Block #2 (Computer)	1---2---3	YES / NO	1---2---3	1---2---3	
Block #3 (Math)	1---2---3	YES / NO	1---2---3	1---2---3	
Block #4 (Language Arts)	1---2---3	YES / NO	1---2---3	1---2---3	

NAME: DATE:

Class/Hour	Polite and Calm	Homework: Overdue?	Works Well with Others	On Task?	Teacher Initials and Comments
Block #1 (Social Studies)	1---2---3	YES / NO	1---2---3	1---2---3	
Block #2 (Computer)	1---2---3	YES / NO	1---2---3	1---2---3	
Block #3 (Math)	1---2---3	YES / NO	1---2---3	1---2---3	
Block #4 (Language Arts)	1---2---3	YES / NO	1---2---3	1---2---3	

159

NAME: DATE:

Class/Hour	Polite and Calm	Homework: Overdue?	Works Well with Others	On Task?	Teacher Initials and Comments
	1---2---3	YES / NO	1---2---3	1---2---3	
	1---2---3	YES / NO	1---2---3	1---2---3	
	1---2---3	YES / NO	1---2---3	1---2---3	
	1---2---3	YES / NO	1---2---3	1---2---3	

NAME: DATE:

Class/Hour	Polite and Calm	Homework: Overdue?	Works Well with Others	On Task?	Teacher Initials and Comments
	1---2---3	YES / NO	1---2---3	1---2---3	
	1---2---3	YES / NO	1---2---3	1---2---3	
	1---2---3	YES / NO	1---2---3	1---2---3	
	1---2---3	YES / NO	1---2---3	1---2---3	

160

Please circle the appropriate number of below.

 **SCHOOL CARD**

Date: _____

Goals	Before Lunch		After Lunch	
On Task				
Staying in Seat When I'm Supposed to				
Listening				
Following Directions				

Please circle the appropriate number of below.

 **SCHOOL CARD**

Date: _____

Goals	Before Lunch		After Lunch	
On Task				
Staying in Seat When I'm Supposed to				
Listening				
Following Directions				

161

Please circle the appropriate number of  below.

 SCHOOL CARD

Date: _____

Goals	Before Lunch		After Lunch	

Please circle the appropriate number of  below.

 SCHOOL CARD

Date: _____

Goals	Before Lunch		After Lunch	

References

The following references were used in the creation of this manual:

American Academy of Pediatrics (1998). Guidelines for Effective Discipline. *Pediatrics, 101,* 723-728.

American Psychiatric Association (1994). *Diagnostic and Statistical Manual for mental Disorders* (4ᵗʰ Edition). New York: APA.

Barkley, R. A. (1998). *Attention-Deficit Hyperactivity Disorder: A Handbook for Diagnosis and Treatment, Second Edition.* New York: Guildford Press.

Barkley, R. A. (2000). *Taking Charge of ADHD, Revised Edition: The Complete, Authoritative Guide for Parents.* New York: Guildford Press.

Barkley, R. A. (2002). *ADHD and the Nature of Self-Control.* New York: Guildford Press.

Barkley, R. A., & Murphy, K. (1998). Attention-*Deficit Hyperactivity Disorder: A Clinical Workbook, Second Edition.* New York: Guildford Press.

Bender, W. (1994). *Understanding ADHD: A Practical Guide for Parents and Teachers.* New Jersey: Prentice Hall.

Bower, M. E., Knutson, J. F. & Winebarger, A. (2002) *Disciplinary history, adult disciplinary attitudes, and risk for abusive parenting.* Journal of Community Psychology

Bower, M.E., Winebarger, A.A. & Knutson, J.F. (July, 1998). *Disciplinary Experiences, Disciplinary Attitudes, and Risk for Abusive Parenting.* Paper Presented at the Biennial Meeting, International Society for the Study of Behavior Development, Berne, Switzerland.

Capaldi, D. M., Pears, K. C., Patterson, G. R., & Owen, L. D. (2003). Continuity of parenting practices across generations in an at-risk sample: A prospective comparison of direct and mediated associations. *Journal of Abnormal Child Psychology, 31,* 127-142.

Chamberlain, P. (2003). The Oregon Multidimensional Treatment Foster Care model: Features, outcomes, and progress in dissemination. In S. Schoenwald & S. Henggeler (Series Eds.) Moving evidence-based treatments from the laboratory into clinical practice. *Cognitive and Behavioral Practice, 10,* 303-312.

Eddy, J. M., Reid, J. B., & Fetrow, R. A. (2000). An elementary-school based prevention program targeting modifiable antecedents of youth delinquency and violence: Linking the Interests of Families and Teachers (LIFT). *Journal of Emotional and Behavioral Disorders, 8,*165-176.

Eddy, J. M., Reid, J. B., Stoolmiller, M., & Fetrow, R. A. (2003). Outcomes during middle school for an elementary school-based preventive intervention for conduct problems: Follow-up results from a randomized trial. *Behavior Therapy, 34,* 535-552.

Eddy. J. M., Fisher, P. A., & Winebarger, A. A. (2000). *WBC Attention Camp Program Staff Training Manual.* Grand Haven, MI.: Western Behavioral Consulting.

164

Fisher, P. A., Eddy. J. M., & Winebarger, A. A. (2000). *WBC Attention Camp Program Social Skills Curriculum.* Grand Haven, MI.: Western Behavioral Consulting.

Forgatch, M. S., & Patterson, G. R. (1989). *Parents And Adolescents Living Together Part 2: Family Problem Solving.* Eugene, OR: Castalia.

Forgatch, M. S., Bullock, B. M., & Patterson, G. R. (2004). From theory to practice: Increasing effective parenting through role-play. In H. Steiner (Ed.), *Handbook Of Mental Health Interventions In Children And Adolescents: An Integrated Developmental Approach* (pp. 782-812). New York: Jossey-Bass.

Hibbs, E. & Jensen, P. (1996). *Psychosocial Treatments for Child and Adolescent Disorders: Empirically Based Strategies for Clinical Practice.* Washington: American Psychological Association.

Kazdin, A. E. (1989). *Behavior Modification in Applied Settings.* Pacific Grove, CA: Brooks/Cole Publishing.

Kentucky Department of Education (2000). *Guidelines for the Effective Use of Time-Out.* http://www.state.ky.us.

Knutson, J. F., DeGarmo, D. S., & Reid, J. B. (2004). Social disadvantage and neglectful parenting as precursors to the development of antisocial and aggressive child behavior: Testing a theoretical model. *Aggressive Behavior, 30,* 187-205.

Leve, L. D., Winebarger, A. A., Fagot, B. I., Reid, J. B., & Goldsmith, H. H. (1998). Environmental and genetic variance in children's observed and reported maladaptive behavior. *Child Development, 182, 1190-1199.*

Leve, L. D., Winebarger, A. A., Goldsmith, H. H., Fagot, B. I., & Reid, J. B. (1995, May). *Environmental influences on observed parent-child interactions: A twin study.* Paper presented at the International Twin Congress, Richmond, VA.

MacKenzie, R. J. (2004). *Setting Limits with Your Strong-Willed Child.*

Marvin, D. (in press). *Attention Camp Activities Curriculum.* Grand Haven, MI: ARW Learning.

Moore, K. J., & Patterson, G. R. (2003). Parent training. In W. O'Donohue, J. E. Fisher & S. C. Hayes (Eds.), *Cognitive Behavior Therapy: Applying Empirically Supported Techniques In Your Practice* (pp. 280-287). New York: John Wiley & Sons.

Nelson, C. M. (1997). *Effective Use of Timeout.* Kentucky Department of Education.

Patterson G. R. (1980). *Coercive Family Process.* Eugene, OR: Castalia.

Patterson, G. R. (1976). *Living With Children: New Methods For Parents And Teachers* (revised ed.). Champaign, IL: Research Press.

Patterson, G. R., & Forgatch, M. S. (1987). *Parents And Adolescents: I. Living Together.* Eugene, OR: Castalia.

Patterson, G. R., Reid, J. B., & Eddy, J. M. (2002). A brief history of the Oregon Model. In J. B. Reid, G. R. Patterson, & J. Snyder (Eds.), *Antisocial Behavior In Children And Adolescents: A Developmental Analysis And Model For Intervention* (pp. 3-21). Washington, DC: American Psychological Association.

Sundberg, N. D., Winebarger, A. A., & Taplin, J. (2002). *Introduction to Clinical Psychology: Evolving Practice, Theory and Research.* Saddle River, NJ: Prentice Hall.

Winebarger, A. A. (1994). *Child perceptions of, and responses to parental discipline and reward behaviors: A twin study.* Unpublished doctoral dissertation, University of Oregon, Eugene.

Winebarger, A. A. (1996, April). *A practical guide to Attention Deficit Hyperactivity Disorder behavioral management systems.* Paper presented at the annual UPLIFT conference, Cheyenne, WY.

Winebarger, A. A. (1996, Nov*). A practical guide to Attention Deficit Hyperactivity Disorder.* Paper presented at the annual Wyoming Governor's Super Conference on Disability Issues, Casper, WY.

Winebarger, A. A., & Poston, W. S. C., (2000). What everyone should know when shopping for a therapist: A survival manual. In A. A. Winebarger, W. S. C. Poston, & C. L. Ruby (Eds.) *Choosing A Therapist: A Practical Guide To The House Of Mirrors.* Cheyenne, WY: Wild Horse Publishing.

Winebarger, A. A., Fisher, P. A., & Eddy. J. M. (2000). *WBC Attention Camp Parenting Skills Enhancement Curriculum.* Grand Haven, MI.: Western Behavioral Consulting.

Winebarger, A. A., Leve, L. D., Reid, J. B., & Goldsmith, H. H. (1995, March). Shared environmental influences on observed compliance in twins. In H. H. Goldsmith (Chair), *Extending developmental behavioral genetics: New findings, new perspectives.* Symposium conducted at the 61st biennial meeting of the Society for Research in Child Development, Indianapolis.

Winebarger, A. A., Schaughency, E. A., McCone, D., Phillips, M., & Vierling, S. (1991, August). *Predicting conduct problems in ADHD children and clinic controls from parental discipline and adjustment.* Paper presented at the annual convention of the American Psychological Association, San Francisco, CA.

Wright, J. (2002). Time out from reinforcement. *Resources to Help Kids Learn.* http://www.interventioncentral.org.

Index